THE KEYS OF FAITH AND HOPE

ROBERT AND KATHY KELSEY

IUNIVERSE, INC.
NEW YORK   BLOOMINGTON

The Keys of Faith and Hope
The Keys to the Kingdom of God Series

Scriptures and Bible verses in this book are from Biblesoft's PC Study Bible Version 4.2B and the following Bibles: The Message Bible, AMP (The Amplified Version), NIV (New International Version), NAS (New American Standard).

All scriptures are from the King James Version of the Bible, unless otherwise noted.

iUniverse books may be ordered through booksellers or by contacting:

iUniverse
1663 Liberty Drive
Bloomington, IN 47403
www.iuniverse.com
1-800-Authors (1-800-288-4677)

ISBN: 978-1-4502-0881-9 (pbk)
ISBN: 978-1-4502-0883-3 (cloth)
ISBN: 978-1-4502-0882-6 (ebook)

Printed in the United States of America

iUniverse rev. date: 3/8/10

I WILL GIVE YOU THE KEYS TO THE KINGDOM OF HEAVEN

MATTHEW 16:19

THE KEYS OF FAITH AND HOPE

A Special Thanks

Our special thanks to all of you who have blessed us these past years by mentoring us and encouraging us to keep doing those things that God has asked us to do. You have led and directed us by your words, your actions, and your examples. Because you kept the faith, that example allowed us to follow in your footsteps and become an example to others.

DEDICATION

Going to church does not make you a Christian unless you go there with an open heart to seek God.

Christians are by no means perfect. They are only forgiven; saved by the blood of Jesus; thus making them perfect in God's eyes.

You cannot serve God and mammon (Matthew 6:24).

Most Christians have just enough religion to make them miserable, and not enough faith to make them happy. They can't enjoy serving the pleasures of sin because they know better, and they can't enjoy serving the Lord because they are not willing to serve Him all of the way.

This book is dedicated to all of you who know Jesus Christ as your personal Lord and Savior and have a desire to experience a closer relationship with Him.

Our prayer is that God will use this book to bring you to understand that God loves you, has you on His mind and wants you to have "the good life," that He has prearranged and made ready for you to live. (Ephesians 2:10 AMP)

Your new life in Christ is God's gift to you, and what you do with that life is your gift to God!

CONTENTS

INTRODUCTION

When I started writing *The Key of Love*, the idea of writing another book never entered my mind. While studying and doing research for the book, I made a rather extensive file of notes on faith and hope and how to live by faith for my own use but not with any intention of using it for the outline of another book.

One of the keys that I have learned when obeying and doing what God has for you, is that He never reveals any more information to you than what you need right then. I suppose that if I knew that I was to write more than one book back when I started *The Key of Love*, I probably would never have started that first one as it took me quite a while for me to believe in myself; that I had what it takes to do it because "… all things are possible to him that believeth" (Mark 9:23).

The key was learning that the Holy Spirit was living on the inside of me and He had a desire to be in partnership with me in doing what God had asked me to do. He was there to lead me and guide me into all Truth. I learned that God's Word is Truth and if I wanted to understand that Truth I had to learn to have a relationship with the Holy Spirit and let Him lead me into all Truth.

My purpose in writing this book is to get you from where you are with God to where God wants you to be—to give you knowledge of the revealed will of God, by which you may enter into that life that pleases God—in the shortest possible amount of time. I want you to move in one day what took me months to go.

In Matthew 20:14, we see where those employees who were hired at the end of the day received the same wage as those who started in the early morning. It will be the same with you if you will hire on with the Kingdom of God. The same benefits, the same grace, the same wisdom and the same revelation knowledge that I worked for all these years is yours when you hire on and seek His Kingdom and His righteousness (His way of doing and being right), because when you do, God will do the rest (Matthew 6:33) Amplified Bible.

The Keys of Faith and Hope is not meant to be a fast read but is designed to be a study guide to get you from where you are to where God wants you to be, so have your Bible and a notebook with you as you read and take the time to look up and study the numerous references to scripture herein, as well as – cross-references, which appear in parentheses following many of the Bible quotations. Take your Bible and read each scripture and those before it and after it several times. Study it, meditate on it, and let the Word of God be your final judge (I Thessalonians 5:21).

If you desire to experience a closer walk with God, you can come to know God and understand just how much He loves and cares for you. Ask the Holy Spirit to help you as you study (John 16:13). God has sent the Holy Spirit into your life to guide you unto all truth, to guide you through life, and to guide you as you walk into the future. So take full advantage of all that God has provided for you to make your life everything that He has created it to be. He sees everything; He knows every nook, corner, and bend in the road of life. If you will reach out and take His hand, He will lead you on shortcuts that will save you time and energy. It's your choice. (Matthew 20:14).

To understand God, one must understand that there are keys to the kingdom of God that unlock the mystery of how we can know the revealed will of God and achieve what He has planned for us.

God has given you those keys, and your failure to live by faith is to condemn yourself to a lower plane of existence than the one that God created you to experience.

1

THE KEYS TO THE KINGDOM OF GOD

In Matthew 16:17–19, Peter made this great confession:

> Thou are the Christ, the Son of the living God.
>
> And Jesus answered and said unto him, Blessed art thou, Simon Bar-jona: for flesh and blood hath not revealed it unto thee, but my Father which is in heaven.
>
> And I say also unto thee, that thou are Peter, and upon this rock I will build my church; and the gates of hell shall not prevail against it.
>
> And I will give unto thee the keys of the kingdom of heaven: and whatever thou shalt bind on earth shall be bound in heaven: and whatsoever thou shalt loose on earth shall be loosed in heaven.

Just as Jesus prophesied that His church would be built on Peter's revelation that Jesus was indeed the Son of God, your perception of who you are in Him will always carry you through to victory.

What did Jesus mean when He said, "the keys to the Kingdom"? His use of the plural word *keys* means there is more than one that will unlock all of the doors and not just one or two. *Key*, from the Greek word *kleis*, is used to mean knowledge of the revealed will of God by which men enter into the life that pleases God. Keys represent power and authority. In Matthew 28:18–20 AMP, Jesus said that:

… All authority (all power of rule) in heaven and on earth has been given to Me.

Go then and make disciples of all nations, baptizing them into the name of the Father and of the Son and of the Holy Spirit,

Teaching them to observe everything that I have commanded you, and behold, I am with you all the days (perpetually, uniformly, and on every occasion), to the [very] close and consummation of the age. Amen (so let it be).

II Corinthians 5:20 AMP tells us that "we are Christ's ambassadors." We are God's ambassadors, His personal representatives here on the earth, representing the Kingdom of God, which is the Church. He has delegated His power and authority to us to go out and make His appeal to the world to be saved through us as believers in Jesus Christ. And He has given us the authority, power, and wisdom to know how to operate as ambassadors to Christ, His personal representatives here on the earth.

We have been given what has been referred to as the Great Commission (Matthew 28:19). The word *commission* tells us what it is all about: "co" (meaning *joint*) and "mission" (meaning *assignment*). It's a joint assignment between God and us, the Church. When Jesus gave the commandment to "Go and make disciples of all nations," He was not only speaking of the assignment that we are to carry out; but also to the assignment that He had already started.

Our responsibility is to carry out the work that Jesus has already started. We are His disciples, and when God decides that He wants to do something here on the earth, He first looks for a willing person who will do His will. His will is to seek and to save the lost, and He has already chosen us to make it happen (Ephesians 1:4).

He has equipped you with all that you will need to get the job done. He has blessed you "with all spiritual blessings in heavenly places in Christ" (Ephesians 1:3), and He expects you to take what has been freely given to you and use it as it was intended to be used and pass it along to others.

Because of Jesus' sacrifice on the cross, "we are more than conquerors through Him that loved us" (Romans 8:37). As more than conquerors our assignment is not only to conquer the enemy but to also conquer everything in the area of the assignment that God has given us.

To do this means living a life of grace, not performance. It means loving others like He does—unconditionally and unwaveringly. When you are willing to live your life and conform to His nature and give God your best, you will succeed.

My goal in writing this book is to show you how to get from where you are to where God wants you to be, and the answer to that is found in Psalms 25:4–5:

> Show me thy ways, O Lord, teach me thy paths.
> Lead me in thy truth, and teach me.
> "Show me your ways, O Lord, and teach me your paths."

How much simpler can it be? All that God is asking you to do is to ask; Lord, teach me! We are instructed in Hebrews 4:16 to:

> . . . come boldly unto the throne of grace, that we may obtain mercy, and find grace to help in time of need.

God is inviting you to His throne for advice, counsel, and instruction. He is waiting for you to allow Him to be your teacher, which will require you to spend quality time with Him. If you never give Him any of your time, how else can God show you his ways? If you will take the time to meditate on God's Word, you will discover that God longs to teach you. He longs to show you how to be a winner in the life that He has called you to. You only need to ask and then be still long enough to hear Him. He will almost always wait for you to start the conversation, but you must be willing to wait on Him for His response. The results will always be extremely beneficial to you (Isaiah 40:31).

In Psalms 25:14 (AMP), David tells us "the secret" of allowing God to reveal His deep things to us:

> The secret of the sweet satisfying companionship of the Lord have they who fear, revere and worship Him and he will show them His covenant and reveal to them its deep inner meaning.

Did you notice the three things that are required of you? He requires you to fear Him, to revere Him, and to worship Him. Then He will show you His covenant and reveal to you its deep inner meaning.

When God's covenant is being revealed to you, it will have a profound impact upon your life, and you will approach that life with a different attitude than the one you have now. And when you realize that God is your teacher and He is teaching you His ways, it will give you a whole different attitude about life. That is why there should be nothing more important than talking with the Lord each day. When you are in tune with Him, He will set your course and give you specific directions.

God will not just talk to you to hear Himself speak. He has spoken things into existence for your benefit, His purposes and His plans, and He greatly desires to share them with you. He tells us in Jeremiah 33:3 AMP to "Call unto me, and I will answer thee, and show thee great and mighty things...."

God desires to have an intimate relationship with you, and to do so you must be in constant conversation with Him in your spirit, which will profit you by revealing to you God's hidden wisdom. Proverbs 20:27 tells us that "The spirit of man is the candle of the Lord, searching all the inward parts of the belly."

There are a lot of things that you can give your attention to, but God gave you a spiritual antenna to pick up on what's more real than what you see with your eyes and hear with your ears (John 16:13).

God is a spirit. Man is a spirit-being. God contacts us, deals with us, and leads us through our spirits. He does not communicate directly through our minds, because the Holy Spirit does not dwell in our minds, and God does not contact us through our bodies either. According to Romans 8:16, "The Spirit itself beareth witness with our spirit, that we are the children of God."

That witness is called our "inward witness," and that is how God communicates with us. God's Spirit "bears witness" with our spirit. You don't know how you know, but you just know it down on the inside of you. "He that believeth on the Son of God hath the witness in himself...." (I John 5:10).

The way that God confirms the most important thing that can ever happen to you, is also the way He leads His children: by the inward witness. Probably the most important aspect of your life—becoming a child of God— is confirmed to you by God's Holy Spirit bearing witness with your spirit that you have been born again (Romans 8:16). I said that to help you understand that the number one way God leads His children is through the inward witness.

I relate that inward witness to a stoplight on the inside of me. If I have the green light, I feel an assurance that everything is going okay. A yellow light warns me to be careful and look around for signs that there is danger around. And a red light is a check in my spirit that acts like a stop sign telling me not to proceed forward on that path.

It will take time and training to know what you are feeling in your spirit, but you have the Holy Spirit in you to lead and guide you.

One way to get to the place that you want to be is to make positive confessions of faith based on the Word of God. You will find several of these confessions scattered throughout this book and they are there to be a guide on how to put them together for you benefit.

Confess: I am a child of God. I have been born again. I am born of the Spirit of God. God's Spirit bears witness with my spirit that I am a child of God. For as many as are led by the Spirit of God, they are the sons of God. I am a child of God; therefore, the Spirit of God leads me and guides me into all truth, and He is leading me now. I trust Him, the Greater One that lives in me. He will rise up big in me. He will give illumination to my mind. He will give directions to my spirit, for I am a child of God. I am being led by the Spirit of God. And the Spirit of God leads me, first of all, through that inward witness (Romans 8:16; I John 5:10; John 14:16–18, 15:26, 16:13).

Is it no wonder that David constantly cried out to God to be taught His ways? (Psalms 24:4–5, 27:11, 86:11, 119:12, 26, 33, 64, 66, 68, 108, 124, 135, 143:10). And we can plainly see that God responded to that hunger by making David [and everybody who will make the decision to ask and believe] a promise. "I will instruct thee and teach thee in the way which thou shalt go: I will guide thee with my eye" (Psalms 32:8).

When God is showing you what to do and how to do it, if you follow those instructions, there's no way that you can fail.

In John 10:7, 9, Jesus told His disciples, "… I am the door of the sheep.… I am the door: by me if any man enter in, he shall be saved, and shall go in and out, and find pasture." This tells us that Jesus is the "door" for us to enter into all of the good things that God has provided for us in His Word (John 14:6).

Jesus opened the door between God and man when He went to the cross at Calvary. Because Jesus shed His blood, we can step into righteousness, and we can walk in redemption and forgiveness of our sin. Because of the stripes that we laid upon Jesus' back, we can walk in healing and divine health. Jesus is the key, the open door for us, giving us access to all of God's provisions (II Corinthians 5:21; I John 1:9; I Peter 2:24).

In John 14:6 AMP, Jesus tells that "… I am the way, the truth, and the life: no one cometh unto the Father, but by Me." (I John 5:11 - 12) Jesus is the way—the open door—to the father. An open door says, "Yes, you may come in." Jesus is the "yes" for all, the open door that enables us to possess all of the promises of the Father (II Corinthians 1:20).

That tells me that if He is the way, I should be doing things His way. I should be allowing the life that the Word of God will bring into my life as a new creature in Christ (II Corinthians 5:17) to flow through me. I should allow the Word of God to clear my mind of all selfish thoughts and cause me to reject the life of that selfish, self-centered person who does nothing but think about myself. In turn, I will be able to reach out and do what God has called me to do, knowing that He will reach out to me and bring answers that I could never get anywhere else which will bring me joy unspeakable.

Can't you just picture in your mind Jesus standing in the street holding a big sign with an arrow on it and a message that says, "This way to salvation, peace, happiness, holiness, healing, and prosperity. Come have your every need met in abundance."?

To get yourself into position to receive all that God is you must know and accept that Jesus is "the truth" (John 14:6). "Thy Word is truth" (John 17:17). "In the beginning [before all time] was the Word (Christ), and the Word was with God, and the Word was God Himself. He was present originally with God" (John 1:1–2; I John 1:1–3 AMP).

> And the Word (Christ) became flesh (human, incarnate) and tabernacle (fixed His tent of flesh, lived awhile) among us; and we [actually] saw His glory (His honor, His majesty), such glory as an only begotten son receives from his father, full of grace (favor, loving-kindness) and truth. (John 1:14 AMP; Isaiah 40:5; Luke 3:5–6).
>
> … If you abide in My word [hold fast to My teachings and live in accordance with them], you are truly My disciples.
> And you will know the Truth, and the Truth will set you free (John 8:31–32 AMP).

Did you notice that if you will abide (live in) God's Word, hold fast to His teachings, and live in accordance with them, you will be one of His disciples His disciplined ones). Then, and only then, will the Truth set you free.

This takes action on your part; it won't just fall on you as you sit in the shade and sip a cool one. You must discipline yourself and spend quality time in the Word and with God on a daily basis, because Jesus is "the life" (John 14:6).

> In Him was life; and the life was the light of men.
> And the Light shines on in the darkness, for the darkness has never overpowered it [put out or absorbed it or appropriated it and is unreceptive to it]. (John 1:4–5 AMP)

Life here in the Greek is *Zoe* which means "eternal life or God's life." It is God's nature. It is life as God has it—that which the Father has in Himself—

and that which the Incarnate Son has in Himself. It is called eternal life, everlasting life, and sometimes just life. Jesus said: "… I am the light of the world: he that followeth me shall not walk in darkness, but shall have the light of life" (John 8:12).

> He that believeth on the Son of God hath the witness in himself: he that believeth not God hath made him a liar; because he believeth not the record that God gave to his Son.
> And this is the record, that God hath given to us eternal life, and this life is in his Son.
> He that hath the Son hath life; and he that hath not the Son of God hath not life (I John 5:10–12).

Jesus, the Word of God made flesh, has demonstrated to us that He is the way, the truth, and the life and that no man can come to the father but by Him. There is absolutely no other way of gaining access to the Father with the assurance of spending eternity in heaven than to go through Jesus.

Matthew 6:33 (AMP) tells us to "… seek (aim at and strive after) first of all His kingdom and His righteousness (His way of doing and being right), and then all these things taken together will be given you besides."

As Christians, God requires us to seek first all His ways of doing and being right where as religion requires its followers to do what its leaders think or say is right.

As one studies the religions of the world you will find that each one has a different set of rules or interpretations of how its leaders require you to act and live.

Christianity is different from all of the religions of the world in that we have our God living on the inside of us. Our bodies are the temple of the Holy Ghost; we are the temple of the living God, and Christ lives in us (I Corinthians 3:16; 6:19, II Corinthians 6:16; Galatians 2:20; I John 4:15). And we are directed by God in I Corinthians 3:17 NIV to take care of our bodies: "If anyone destroys God's temple, God will destroy him; for God's temple is sacred, and you are that temple."

Remember, God will never turn you away because of who or what you are. There isn't, nor has there ever been but one sin so great that it was not covered by the shed blood of Jesus at the cross of Calvary (Matthew 12:31).

That life can be yours if you will invite Jesus into your life not only as your Lord and Savior but also as your best friend.

If you don't know Jesus as your personal Lord and Savior, I would like to take this opportunity to introduce you to the greatest friend you'll ever have.

As you make this confession, if you will believe with your heart, you will be born again (Romans 10:9–10).

> Jesus, I invite you to come into my life. Forgive me of all my sins. I believe that You died for my sins on the cross and I ask You to come into my heart and make a change in me right now. Jesus, I want to thank You for loving me enough to die for me. I accept all that Your shed blood bought for me on the cross, and I receive You as my Lord and personal Savior. In Jesus' Name, I pray. Amen.

By simply praying this prayer, believing in your heart, and confessing with your mouth that Jesus is your Lord and Savior, you have a whole new life with Jesus that you can look forward to starting right now. Your record is clean before God. Your spirit has been reborn because of Christ's great sacrifice and His love for you. According to 2 Corinthians 5:17, you are now in Christ; you are a new creature: old things (that old sin nature) has passed away, and all things have become new. "Christ lives in you, [then although] your [natural] body is dead by reason of sin and guilt, your spirit is alive because of [the] righteousness [that He imputes to you]." (Romans 8:10 AMP; I Corinthians 3:16, 6:19).

Now God is asking you to "… lay apart all filthiness and superfluity of naughtiness, and receive with meekness the engrafted word, which is able to save your souls" (James 1:21).

Jesus' blood has washed and cleansed you, and God has given you a new robe of righteousness. So be careful not to fall back into that old negative, faithless environment from which you came. It will take a strong act of determination on your part to stay free of those old encumbrances, but it will be well worth it! You must learn to *lay apart* or to deliberately lay down wrong attitudes and habits and push them so far out of range that you won't be able to reach down and pick them up again.

If any old thoughts try to worm their way into your mind, stop them with your mouth. Your mind will always stop working to hear what your mouth has to say. (As an example, silently count to ten, and when you get to five, speaks your name out loud. Notice that you're counting stopped to hear what your mouth was saying.) As such, when the devil puts thoughts about your old life into your mind, simply tell him about your new life in Christ. Tell him that his hold over you has been broken by the blood of Jesus and that you are a new creature in Christ. Tell him that "in Christ, old things are passed away, behold all things are become new" (II Corinthians 5:17). This is the process of resisting the devil, and when you continually do that, he will flee from you as if in terror (James 4:7).

Next, start by asking the Holy Spirit to show you if there are any wrong attitudes from your past that you are still carrying around in your life. He will not only show them to you, but He will give you the power to remove them from your life. That's God's grace—God's power and ability extended to you—in action in your life (II Corinthians 12:9; Romans 8:11).

Everything that you do has its basis on the way you think; if you don't change the way you think, you won't effectively alter your behavior. Wrong thinking equals wrong actions. The only way to permanently change what you do is to renew your mind with the Word of God.

> My son, attend to my words; incline thine ear unto my sayings.
>
> Let them not depart from thine eyes; keep them in the midst of thine heart.
>
> For they are life unto those that find them, and health to all their flesh (Proverbs 4:20–22).

God's Word ministers to the total man. His Word (Jesus) is our wisdom, righteousness, sanctification, and redemption (I Corinthians 1:30).

This is why it is so important for us to use our words in a positive way—a way that will produce liberty, healing, and health that the Word of God said it would.

Most people use their words to hold themselves in bondage by speaking contrary to God's Word. In John 10:10, we are told that the devil came only that he may kill, steal, and destroy. He does that by getting us to speak words that he has said himself. He gets us to quote what he has said about us, and in so doing, we establish on the earth the words that the enemy has said.

In Matthew 6:10, Jesus directed the Apostles to pray: "Thy will be done in earth, as it is in heaven." When we begin to establish the things that God said and establish His Word on this earth, then we will rise to a new level of faith and then we will see God's will being done here on earth. Then we will walk in the level of life where we release the ability of God by the words of our mouth. And this is what will cause His Word and His power to become available to us. God's Word is forever settled in heaven, and it is up to us to establish His Word here upon the earth (Psalm 119:89).

To renew your mind, I also encourage you to start today and make this confession of faith the first thing every morning for the rest of your life, because faith in God and the things of God come to you by hearing the Word of God.

Good morning, Lord Jesus. For this is the day I again declare that You are my Lord [referring to Your majesty, honor, authority, and sovereignty]. I submit this day and all that it contains to you, for this is the day which the Lord has made; I will rejoice and be glad in it, for the joy of the Lord is my strength. I am strong in the Lord and the power of His might, and I can do all things through Christ which strengthens me. For You, Lord, are at work in me, creating in me the power and the desire, both to will and to work for Your good pleasure. (Romans 10:9; Psalm 27:14, 118:24; Nehemiah 8:10; Ephesians 6:10; Philippians 2:13, 4:13)

Knowing what the keys are and how to use them is one of the greatest avenues that you can go down to bring that into reality.

The two keys that I will deal with in this book primarily are the keys of faith and hope.

Faith or faithfulness is so esteemed by God that it is listed in I Corinthians 13:13 where Paul writes: "And now abideth faith, hope, charity [love] ..." This fruit of the spirit (Galatians 5:22; Ephesians 5:9) is a part of the eternal nature of God, and God desires that you be so filled with that fruit that it would be a reflection of you in this world. The Bible stresses that God is faithful (I Corinthians 1:9) and utterly dependable.

Numbers 23:19 (NIV) says, "God is not a man, that he should lie, nor a son of man, that he should change his mind" (Titus 1:2). And Hebrews 13:8 (AMP) tells us, "Jesus Christ (the Messiah) is [always] the same, yesterday, today, [yes] and forever (to the ages)."

And God desires that as He is we should be also! II Corinthians 5:7 (AMP) says, "For we walk by faith [we regulate our lives and conduct ourselves by our conviction or belief respecting man's relationship to God and divine things, with trust and holy fervor; thus we walk] not by sight or appearance."

WHAT IS FAITH?

Faith is defined in Hebrews 11:1 as "... the substance of things hoped for, the evidence of things not seen." Whereas the Amplified Bible gives us a more complete definition and defines faith as "... the assurance (the confirmation, the title deed) of things [we] do not see and the conviction of their reality [faith perceiving as real fact what is not revealed to the senses]."

The word *faith* here comes from the Greek words, *pistis, pisteoos,* and *hee,* meaning conviction of the truth of anything, belief.

Colossians 1:4 from the Amplified Bible defines faith as "… [the leaning of your entire human personality on Him in absolute trust and confidence in His power, wisdom, and goodness] and of the love which you [have and show] for all the saints (God's consecrated ones)."

In turn, Romans 10:17 (AMP) tells us that "… faith comes by hearing [what is told], and what is heard comes by the preaching [of the message that came from the lips] of Christ (the Messiah Himself)."

There is the *logos*, the written Word, and the *rhema*, the quickened Word to you, known as revelation knowledge.

Real faith comes when you hear that personal Word for yourself and you allow it becomes a revelation to you directly from God. You not only get this kind of faith from hearing the personal Word of God to you but also from hearing that written Word of God preached like it is happening today (Matthew 16:17).

There are two sides to Romans 10:17: Faith in both God and the things of God come from hearing the Word of God. "Faith comes by hearing" tells us that anything that we hear enough times will be perceived as the truth in our spirits. In short, if we hear a lie enough times, we will believe it as the truth. The devil knows this, and he uses it to destroy lives on a wholesale scale. One of his best assets is the news media. Take a little time and study world history for the past hundred years and notice how the news media, controlled by ungodly people, has destroyed the lives of millions of people. And it is still happening today. Is it any wonder why we are told in Hosea 4:6 that: "My people are destroyed for lack of knowledge: because thou hast rejected knowledge.…"? This is why Paul told the Corinthians in II Corinthians 13:1 that "… In the mouth of two or three witnesses shall every word be established." To depend on only one witness for the truth is just opening the door for trouble.

It is good for us to read the Word of God on a daily basis, but when God makes it a reality to you by a revelation, it simply means it was moved from your head into your heart.

Don't fall into the trap of thinking that you have to read a specific number of pages or chapters a day. It is better to read only a few verses and spend quality time meditating on them until you get a revelation of what God is saying than to read several pages and not get anything out of them.

Confess: In Him was life, and that life is the light of man. That life is in me; that life is developing my spirit, and I have the mind of Christ. I have that same anointing on my mind that Jesus has on His mind, and I have the wisdom of God, and revelation knowledge flows into me continually (John 1:3; I Corinthians 1:30, 2:16; James 1:5).

You establish yourself in the Word by making confessions of faith based on Mark 11:24, "… What things soever ye desire when you pray, believe that ye receive them and ye shall have them." Just do like God did when He created this world. He called those things that were not as though they were, or with His Words He made something out of nothing (Romans 4:17). It is your words spoken over and over that cause your faith to develop and the manifestation of God's Word to develop in your life.

We have God's Word on it. The scriptures are filled with the promise of God's help to withstand the trials in life and live in victory.

> No weapon that is formed against thee shall prosper; and every tongue that shall rise against thee in judgment thou shalt condemn. This is the heritage of the servants of the Lord, and their righteousness is of me, saith the Lord (Isaiah 54:17).

> What shall we then say to these things? If God be for us, who can be against us? (Romans 8:31)

> The Lord is my light and my salvation; whom shall I fear? The Lord is the strength of my life; of whom shall I be afraid?
> Though an host should encamp against me, my heart shall not fear: though war should rise against me, in this will I be confident. (Psalm 27:1, 3)

As a believer, God's word reveals several truths:

You are redeemed: "Neither by the blood of goats and calves, but by his own blood he entered in once into the holy place, having ordained eternal redemption for us" (Hebrews 9:12).

You are a new creation in Christ: "Therefore if any man be in Christ, he is a new creature: old things are passed away; behold all things are become new" (II Corinthians 5:17).

You are the righteousness of God in Christ Jesus: "For he hath made him to be sin for us who knew no sin; that we might be made the righteousness of God in him" (II Corinthians 5:21).

God will never leave you nor forsake you (Hebrews 13:5): "Fear thou not; for I am with thee; be not dismayed; for I am thy God: I will strengthen thee; yea, I will help thee; yea, I will uphold thee with the right hand of my righteousness" (Isaiah 41:10).

God doesn't lie: "God is not a man, that he should lie; neither the son of man, that he should repent: hath he said, and shall he not do it? Or hath he spoken, and shall he not make it good?" (Numbers 23:19).

Your faith in God can overcome the world: "For whatsoever is born of God overcometh the world: and this is the victory that overcometh the world, even our faith" (I John 5:4).

All of the power that Jesus has is yours: "And Jesus came and spake unto them, saying, All power is given unto me in heaven and in earth" (Matthew 28:18).

Your faith is your key to God's best in your life. What you choose to do with it will determine just how far you can go with God and how much success you will have in life.

Remember: "… whatever does not originate and proceed from faith is sin [whatever is done without a conviction of its approval by God is sinful]" (Romans 14:23 AMP).

WHAT IS HOPE?

Hope is the blueprint that faith works from. Hope is more than just wanting change. Hope causes that change to happen. Hope is a gift from God. Hope lacks substance until it is filled with faith. Hope is only a goal-setter. But like your righteousness, you can't buy it or earn it; you must simply receive it by faith. And once you have received it, you give it away. Hope declared and hope demonstrated is what allows God to do the miraculous.

Hope is from the Greek, *elpis,* meaning, "expectation whether of good or of ill." Hope is the seed, and it is the beginning of every good thing in our lives.

> But hope [the object of] which is seen is not hope. For how can one hope for what he already sees? (Romans 8:24 AMP)

Hope gives birth to the overcoming life, because it always believes for the best, even in the face of the worst circumstances. Hope is much more than just a wish, a yearning, or a positive outlook, because it is based on the promises of God found in His Word, promises that when acted upon will cause God to move on your behalf.

Always remember that God is on your side, and the power of hope is only found in a relationship with Jesus Christ. "For I know the thoughts and plans

I have for you, says the Lord, thoughts and plans for welfare and peace and not for evil, to give you hope in your final outcome" (Jeremiah 29:11).

Romans 5:1–5 (AMP) best exemplifies what our salvation means to us and how important faith, hope, and love are to us as we enter in and allow God to make us complete:

> Therefore, since we are justified (acquitted, declared righteous, and given a right standing with God) through faith, let us [grasp the fact that we] have [the peace of reconciliation to hold and to enjoy] peace with God through our Lord Jesus Christ (the Messiah, the Anointed One).
>
> Through Him also we have [our] access (entrance, introduction) by faith into this grace (state of God's favor) in which we [firmly and safely] stand. And let us rejoice and exult in our hope of experiencing and enjoying the glory of God.
>
> Moreover [let us also be full of joy now!] let us exult and triumph in our troubles and rejoice in our sufferings, knowing that pressure and affliction and hardship produce patient and unswerving endurance.
>
> And endurance (fortitude) develops maturity of character (approved faith and tried integrity). And character [of this sort] produces [the habit of] joyful and confident hope of eternal salvation.
>
> Such hope never disappoints or deludes or shames us, for God's love has been poured out in our hearts through the Holy Spirit Who has been given to us.

Faith, hope, and love are the three essential elements to a successful walk with God, and any one of these will not work without the other two in operation at the same time.

Our hope is our positive expectation and our source of confidence. It is best expounded in II Chronicles 7:14, which Solomon spoke after building the temple:

> If my people, which are called by my name, shall humble [humility] themselves, and pray [prayer], and seek my face [obedience], and turn from their wicked ways; then will I hear from heaven [expectation], and will forgive their sin, and will heal their land. (Notes added by author)

*H*umility, *o*bedience, *p*rayer, and *e*xpectation (which spell *hope*) are a set of behaviors that when practiced will bring about the desired results that every Christian needs.

Humility: God's style is never flashy, pushy, arrogant, inflated with pride, or self-centered (Romans 12:3; I Corinthians 13:4–5; I Peter 5:6 AMP).

Obedience: is simply doing what God is asking us to do. "In all thy ways acknowledge Him, and He will direct thy paths" (Proverbs 3:6).

Prayer: Pray always! Prayer is staying in continual fellowship with God (Luke 21:36; I Thessalonians 5:17).

Expectation: Believe that you will receive. "… being fully persuaded that, what he has promised, he was able also to perform." Stay in expectation that God will faithfully fulfill His Word in your life (Mark 11:24; Isaiah 55:11; Romans 4:21).

Psalms 71:14 tells us: "But I will hope continually, and will yet praise thee more and more." Is there a connection between hope and giving praise to God? (Psalm 34:1; Lamentations 3:25–26; Jeremiah 29:11 AMP).

II Corinthians 5:7 says: "For we walk by faith, not by sight," and we are able to do this because we know that regardless of the circumstances, God is working on our behalf. Nothing in life demonstrates real trust like thanking God when we are in the midst of a crisis (I Thessalonians 5:18) Praise acts like a magnifying glass and it makes God bigger than our problems. This is because our focus changes. Instead of dwelling on our problems and getting discouraged, our faith is released, and we start looking to God for the solutions to our problems.

Confess: But as for me, I will always have hope, because Jesus is my hope. He is filling me with all joy and peace as I put my trust in Him so that I may overflow with hope by the power of the Holy Spirit that lives in me. For the Lord delights in those who fear him and who put their hope in his unfailing love (Psalm 71:14, 147:11; Romans 15:13).

The mercies of God are fresh and new every day. That is why living a life of faith and hope is so important to every Christian. You can't have faith without hope, and that is why the devil and his crowd are out to destroy our hope. The devil knows that hope is the first step to a better life. He knows that without hope we can't have faith and without faith God cannot work in our lives. I can't emphasize enough that this is why the devil works so hard to discourage us and get us to believe that our situation is hopeless. His goal is to steal our hope and he accomplishes that by keeping our focus on where we are right now. He knows that God has great things in store for us but if he can keep us from living a life of expediency in the things that God has for us he has won the battle.

Our goal should be to learn to look beyond where we are right now. We must learn to look not at our circumstances but look at the fact that God has much better things in store for us. We must learn to look beyond where we are right now and see where God wants us to be.

2

THE BASIS OF OUR CHRISTIAN WALK

Faith, hope, and love form the very basis of our Christian walk with God, and this book will deal with the keys of faith and hope. The Amplified Bible depicts them as:

> And so faith, hope, love abide [faith—conviction and belief respecting man's relation to God and divine things; hope—joyful and confident expectation of eternal salvation; love—true affection for God and man, growing out of God's love for and in us], these three; but the greatest of these is love (I Corinthians 13:13) AMP

Hebrews 10:38–39 tells us that "Now the just shall live by faith; but if any man draw back, my soul shall have no pleasure in him." And according to Habakkuk 2:3–4, "But we are not of them who draw back unto perdition; but of them that believe to the saving of the soul." Who are the just? The just, from the Greek *dikaios, dikaia, dikaion,* refer to the righteous, those observing divine and human laws.

And Hebrews 11:6 tells us that "Without faith it is impossible to please Him: for he that cometh to God must believe that he is, and that he is a rewarder of them that diligently seek him."

How do we please God? The first thing that we must do to please God is to have faith that lines up with the Word of God.

The more that we believe God and the more our words and actions conform to His Word, the more He can and will do for us. In short, if we will just sell out for God, diligently seek Him and believe and act upon everything we read in the Bible, then we will be on our way to a life filled with joy and victory in Christ.

Some people are afraid to sell out totally to God. But in order to get all that God has for us, we need to put our lives entirely into the hands of the Lord, requiring Him to teach us how to live and love His way. The fear of being different is causing many people to miss out on one of the greatest experiences that they could ever have, because when one makes a commitment to serve God that is when one really begins to live.

You must be diligent to be rewarded by God, so it should be no surprise that diligence is going to be required in order for you to succeed in every sphere of life. To be successful in life, you will have to adjust your level of commitment and give your full attention to what God has called you to do.

If you are feeling unqualified to accomplish what you have been called to do, just look at the apostles. They were just a bunch of everyday, common people from all walks of life. In fact, common people are often God's first choice, because they are already equipped to a certain degree to face the challenges and difficulties of life.

Proverbs 3:5 instructs us to "Trust in the Lord with all thine heart; and lean not unto thine own understanding." Natural knowledge and understanding are needful in this world that we live in, but if our natural understanding rather than our trust in God becomes the basis for our confidence, we are putting ourselves at a great disadvantage. We have to learn to trust in the Lord and use what we know while leaning only on the Lord and His might.

This is where faith comes in: you cannot hold onto a part of your life and still expect to receive God's best. You have to let go of everything that you have, and only then can God give you everything that He has. To really receive from God, you must be obedient to the leadership of the Holy Spirit and allow Him to be in full control. You have to trust Him, and in order to trust Him, you have to believe Him. That is what faith is—believing God: "For what saith the scripture? Abraham believed God, and it was counted unto him for righteousness" (Hebrews 11:6).

God is no respecter of persons (Acts 10:34), so we know that when we believe God, it will also be counted to us for righteousness (II Corinthians 5:21).

According to Romans 12:2, to get ourselves to that point, we must "… be not conformed to this world: but be ye transformed by the renewing of your mind, that ye may prove what is that good, and acceptable, and perfect, will of God." This is done by spending quality time in the Word of God. You must turn the secular television and radio off and stop doing those nonproductive things that are eating up your time. Today we have the Bible and faith-building teachings available to us on tape, CD, and audio book so that we can listen to it at all times of the day and night. It is up to you to be transformed by the renewing of your mind so that you may prove what is the good, acceptable, and perfect will of God.

This transformation deals with changing your disposition, because the disposition of a person pertains to his or her opinions, attitudes, and outlook. Your disposition includes your mannerisms, tendencies, temper, constitution, inclinations, and propensity, which means it is your frame of mind. As a result, this transformation will affect all of these things.

You must let the Word of Christ dwell in you richly (Colossians 3:16)— no Word, no change; little Word, little change; much Word, much change.

The word *richly*, from the Greek word *plousios,* describes one living in incredible abundance, extreme wealth, enormous affluence, great prosperity, immense riches, magnificent opulence, and extravagant lavishness.

Thus, if you will receive the Word of God in the right way and make it feel at home in your life, it will greatly enrich you spiritually.

For you to get a better understanding, you must understand Isaiah 55: 8–11:

> For my thoughts are not your thoughts, neither are your ways my ways, saith the Lord.
>
> For as the heavens are higher than the earth, so are my ways higher than your ways, and my thoughts than your thoughts.
>
> For as the rain cometh down, and the snow from heaven, and returneth not thither, but watereth the earth, and maketh it bring forth and bud, that it may give seed to the sower, and bread to the eater:
>
> So shall my word be that goeth forth out of my mouth: it shall not return unto me void, but is shall accomplish that which I please, and it shall prosper in the thing whereto I sent it.

One of the hardest lessons to learn from this passage comes from Isaiah 55:8: "For my thoughts are not your thoughts, neither are your ways my ways, saith the Lord."

It is vitally important that we understand that God does not think like us or accomplish things the same way that they are done in the world. For example, God has almost always used common people to build His Kingdom. He hardly ever chooses famous people or noted people to fulfill His plans and purposes on this earth. If you will look back through the history of the

Church and those who choose to live and walk by faith you will not find anybody whom the world would classify and qualified They would almost always be classified as world rejects.

When choosing whom God would use to serve Him, He often chooses the worst the world has to offer and says, "I'm going to do something magnificent through you, and it's all on Me." As we are reminded in Philippians 4:13, "I can do all things through Christ which strengtheneth me." With God in your life, nothing is impossible.

When God chose Samuel to lead the nation of Israel, he was just a young boy. When God looked for someone to kill a giant, He chose a young shepherd boy named David. When it was time for Jesus to come upon the scene, He chose a young girl named Mary to give birth to our Lord and Savior in a stable. (Not what you would call a qualified place for the King of Kings to be born.) When it was time to choose some disciples, He didn't go the local "religious school of the day" and get the most highly qualified students; rather, He chose disciples who knew more about fishing and tax-collecting than about the Word of God. And last of all, when He was looking for someone to write more than half of the New Testament, He chose a man named Saul, who was later renamed Paul, who was one of the most notorious Christian killers of all time! Not one of them would ever have made the list of "Who's Who in the Church" in their time!

If you want to be on God's list, you have to take the attitude that you just don't care what other people think or say about your walk in faith and just go out and do those things that please God. You have to decide that you want to please God more than you want to win the approval of your friends, associates, and peers. And to please God, you must have a desire to help others whenever they need help. It means living your life to be a blessing to others, because faith and love work together: Faith will not work for you if you are not walking in the love of God (John 13:33–35).

The acceptance of God's love means living a life of grace, not performance. It means loving others like He does—unconditionally and unwaveringly. When you are willing to live your life and conform to God's nature and give Him your best, you will succeed.

Love is about the only way that we can show others that we belong to God. God is love (I John 4:8) and He demonstrated His love for us when He gave Jesus, His only begotten Son (John 3:16), and He desires to reveal His love in new ways to others through you.

> … But if we love one other, God abides (lives and remains)
> in us and His love (that love which is essentially His) is

brought to completion (to its full maturity, runs it full course, is perfected) in us! (I John 4:12; Romans 5:5 AMP)

Chances are that God wants you to be right where you are, doing what you are doing, but He wants you to show His love to others. He has positioned you right where you are so that you can pour out His blessings to those around you. You are the open windows of heaven to them, and He is requiring you to live by faith, which will require some action from you. John 14:12 AMP shows us that faith leads to action.

I assure you, most solemnly I tell you, if anyone steadfastly believes in Me, he will himself be able to do the things that I do; and he will do even greater things than these, because I go to the Father.

As you study through this book, you will learn that the same power that flowed through Jesus when He walked on this earth now flows through you to do the same works that He did. The same Holy Spirit who anointed Jesus to fulfill His ministry and who raised Jesus up from the dead has been sent to empower you to do those same works and even greater things (Luke 4:18; Acts 10:28; Romans 8:11).

For you to do these, "even greater things," you are required to take some action. Mark 16:17–18 tells us:

And these signs shall follow them that believe; In my name shall they cast out devils; they shall speak with new tongues;

They shall take up serpents; and if they drink any deadly thing, it shall not hurt them; they shall lay hands on the sick, and they shall recover.

When Christians get to the point that they believe what you have just read and put it into practice in their everyday lives, a great revival will break out—greater than any one of us can even imagine.

Getting from where you are to where God wants you to be is the most important assignment that you can ever tackle, and God has given you all of the power and authority that you will ever need. But you must believe it, and you must act upon that belief (James 2:26).

To do this, we must be in communion with the Holy Spirit on a continual basis. Communion with the Holy Spirit forms the basis of a life of supernatural power and consistency.

II Corinthians 13:14 says "The grace of the Lord Jesus Christ, and the love of God, and the communion of the Holy Ghost, be with you all, Amen."

The word *communion* is the Greek *koinonia,* meaning "partnership and responsibility," among many other things. A good example of partnership is found in Luke 5:7 where Jesus supplied a miraculous catch of fish. Peter realized that he could not handle the catch alone and called for help from the fishermen from a nearby boat. "And they beckoned unto their partners, which were in the other ship, that they should come and help them. And they came, and filled both the ships, so that they begin to sink."

The word *partners* here refers to real, legitimate business partners who were working together to obtain the same goal—catching and selling fish in this instance.

In His earthly ministry, Jesus was in partnership with the Holy Spirit, as we can see in the following verses.

Jesus was conceived of the Holy Spirit (Luke 1:35), empowered by the Holy Spirit (Matthew 3:16; Acts 10:38), and led by the Holy Spirit (Matthew 4:1). Jesus also healed people by the power of the Holy Spirit (Acts 10:38), cast out demons by the power of the Holy Spirit (Matthew 12:28), was resurrected from the dead by the power of the Holy Spirit (Romans 8:11), and was seated at God's right hand in the heavenly places through the power of the Holy Spirit (Ephesians 1:19–20).

How dependant was Jesus on the Holy Spirit? John 5:30–32 AMP gives us insight to this:

> I am able to do nothing from Myself [independently, of My own accord—but only as I am taught by God and as I get His orders]. Even as I hear, I judge [I decide as I am bidden to decide. As the voice comes to Me, so I give a decision], and My judgment is right (just, righteous), because I do not seek or consult My own will [I have no desire to do what is pleasing to Myself, My own aim, My own purpose] but only the will and pleasure of the father Who sent Me.
>
> If I alone testify in My behalf, My testimony is not valid and cannot be worth anything.
>
> There is Another Who testifies concerning Me, and I know and am certain that His evidence on My behalf is true and valid.

Notice that every time we see Jesus in the Gospels, He is working side by side in partnership with the Holy Spirit. He even tells us in verse 30 that He wouldn't initiate anything by Himself, indicating His total dependence on the Holy Spirit. As followers of Jesus Christ, we must also be in partnership with and dependent on the Holy Spirit to accomplish our divine role here on this earth.

According to Proverbs 14:12 AMP, "There is a way that seems right to man and appears straight before him, but the end of it is the way of death." It is when we go out on our own and try to accomplish what God has given us to do that we will oftentimes fall flat on our faces. Without being in partnership with the Holy Spirit, we are never able to accomplish God's best.

Just as the Holy Spirit wants to become your partner, He also wants to assume responsibility for you in this world, but you have to allow Him to do so. You must open your heart to the Spirit of God and allow Him to come in and have an intimate relationship with you, to assume a more active role in your life and to ensure you that you are not alone. And this will only happened when you decide to get to know the Holy Spirit as your most intimate friend and make Him your partner by allowing Him to help you fulfill the responsibilities of your calling in Christ.

You start by inviting the Holy Spirit into your life as your helper, your counselor, your guide, and your partner. You yield yourself to Him—spirit, soul, and body—and you consult with Him before you make a decision or take a single step.

This step requires a very serious commitment on your part. It will require you to know and understand that God is actually living in you. Everywhere you go, everything you see, everything you say, and everything you hear is also being experienced by God. The question that you need to settle is this: does He approve of where you are going, what you are seeing, what you are saying, and what you are hearing?

A really good indication that He doesn't is that you aren't hearing anything from Him.

John 16:13 tells us "Howbeit when he, the Spirit of truth, is come, he will guide you into all truth: for he shall not speak of himself; but whatsoever he shall hear, that shall he speak: and he will show you things to come." Did you notice that "He will guide you into all truth, and He will show you things to come"? Notice, He will! Not he might. But you have to allow Him to do so. God will never force Himself on you.

Jesus is telling us that the Holy Spirit would "… show you things to come." The word *show* is the Greek word *odegeo* and is the word for a guide who shows a traveler the safest way that he should go through an unknown country. This means that the Holy Spirit is your guide. He knows the way that you should go. He understands how to avoid every trap and obstacle along the way. When you are going into an area you've never been before, He wants to show you how to take the safest route. He knows exactly how to get you safely to your destination. The Holy Spirit knows your future and wants to enlighten you with all of the information that you will need in every situation.

Being able to receive revelation knowledge out of a verse of scripture where the natural mind is getting nothing is just one of the many benefits you receive as a child of God.

The Holy Spirit wants to guide you through life. He wants to guide you as you walk into the future. His desire is to reveal to you the truth in all matters and show you things to come.

Just imagine: a farmer knowing what and when to plant his crops, a storekeeper knowing what to order to stock his shelves for next month, a stock broker knowing when to buy and sell stocks, a manufacturer knowing when to speed up or slow down his production line, a fisherman knowing whether to fish or stay home and paint his house.

It is only when you open up your heart to Him that He will come in and do those things that can only be described directly from the Word of God. Unless you allow Him to reveal the truth of God's Word to you, you will never really know what God is telling you.

I Corinthians 2: 9–16 (AMP) gives us a better look at what I am telling you:

> ... What eye has not seen and ear has not heard and has not entered into the heart of man, [all that] God has prepared (made and keeps ready) for those who love Him [who hold Him in affectionate reverence, promptly obeying Him and gratefully recognizing the benefits He has bestowed].
>
> Yet to us God has unveiled and revealed them to and through His Spirit, for the [Holy] Spirit searches diligently, exploring and examining everything, even sounding the profound and bottomless things of God [the divine counsels and things hidden and beyond man's scrutiny].
>
> For what person perceives (knows and understand) what passes through a man's thoughts except the man's own spirit within him? Just so no one discerns (comes to know and comprehend) the thoughts of God except the Spirit of God.
>
> Now we have not received the spirit [that belongs to] the world, but the [Holy] Spirit Who is from God, [given to us] that we might realize and comprehend and appreciate the gifts [of divine favor and blessing so freely and lavishly] bestowed on us by God.

And we are setting these truths forth in words not taught by human wisdom but taught by the [Holy] Spirit, combining and interpreting spiritual truths with spiritual language [to those who possess the Holy Spirit].

But the natural, nonspiritual man does not accept or welcome or admit into his heart the gifts and teachings and revelations of the Spirit of God, for they are folly (meaningless nonsense) to him; and he is incapable of knowing them [of progressively recognizing, and becoming better acquainted with them] because they are spiritually discerned and estimated and appreciated.

But the spiritual man tries all things [he examines, investigates, inquires into, questions, and discerns all things], yet is himself to be put on trial and judged by no one [he can read the meaning of everything, but no one can properly discern or appraise or get an insight into him].

For who has known or understood the mind (the counsels and purposes) of the Lord so as to guide and instruct Him and give Him knowledge? But we have the mind of Christ (the Messiah) and do hold the thoughts (feelings and purposes) of His heart. (Philippians 2:5)

For your own benefit, I would suggest that you read the above verses over and spend time meditating on what they are saying to you about what a great benefit it is to your Christian life to have the Holy Spirit.

Jesus said in John 14:18 that he would not leave us comfortless. For anyone who has made Jesus their Lord and Savior, He is responsible for their daily welfare.

His desire is for you and me to get our instructions from Him on what we should be doing and how to do it. He knows what our future holds, and He is willing to show us things to come so that we may avoid the trials and tribulations that the devil is preparing for us.

God is speaking to us all of the time, but most of the time we are just too busy to listen to what He is saying to us, or we have failed to keep ourselves built up on our most holy faith, by praying in the Holy Ghost. Praying in the spirit is simply your spirit talking directly to God.

God has sent us the Holy Spirit (the Spirit of truth) to guide us into all truth. And if you will allow Him to do so, God will guide you and lead you (John 16:13).

According to Romans 8:14, "For as many as are led by the Spirit of God, they are the sons of God." Do you see the requirements there is to be a son

25

of God? You must allow yourself to be led by the Spirit of God. That is the difference of being a Christian and living like a Christian. Leading a life that would allow the Holy Spirit that lives in you to lead you and guide you into all truth is the key to knowing what God expects of you.

I will say it again: being led by the Holy Spirit is one of the greatest privileges that we receive as children of God. The word *led*, from the Greek word *ago*, describes the act of leading about an animal, such as a cow or a goat, at the end of a rope. The owner would wrap a rope around the animal's neck and then tug or pull until the animal started to follow him. When the animal decided to cooperate and follow that gentle tug, it could then be gently led to where its owner wanted to go with it.

It is the same with you and me; we must pay careful attention to the tugging of the Holy Spirit in our hearts. The Holy Spirit is a gentleman and does not force us to obey Him. He simply prompts us with tugs on our hearts, and He pulls on our spirit to get our attention. Oftentimes, His tugs are so gentle that we almost miss them. Only you can develop sensitivity to the Holy Spirit. But if you will allow Him to do so, He will gently lead you exactly where He wants you to go with your life.

Romans 8:16 tells us that:

"The Spirit itself [Himself] beareth witness with our spirit, that we are the children of God." There is no other way to know that you are a child of God. I John 5:10 explains to us that "He that believeth on the Son of God hath the witness in himself …" The most important aspect of your life is becoming a child of God, and that is confirmed to you by God's Spirit bearing witness to your spirit, that you have become a born again child of God.

You will find that God's No. 1 way to communicate with you is through that inward witness. It is simply a knowing down on the inside of you that God is talking to you. I liken that inward witness to a stoplight. When it is green, I am free to go forward with what I am doing, but if it is yellow, I have a warning to look around and check things out, because there is something dangerous lurking in the shadows. The red light tells me to stop and throw up a hedge of protection around myself, because I am entering into a zone of great danger. Oftentimes, it means only to back up and proceed in a different direction.

I can't tell you the number of times that I have ignored or didn't recognize that red light and have stepped off into some dire circumstances and had to live with the troubles and tribulations that came with it.

I am sure that if you will just stop and think about the last few minutes before a tribulation befell you, there was that inward witness telling you not to do something or to do it differently. An excellent example to study is the number of people who worked in the World Trade Center in New York City on September 11, 2001, that for one reason or another didn't go or were late for work that morning.

It is important for you to know that the real you is not your flesh-and-blood body, it is your spirit man, the real you, the man on the inside. You were created in the image and likeness of God (Genesis 1:26). God is a spirit (John 4:24), and you are a spirit-being made in the image and likeness of God. It was that spirit-being that was born again, not your physical body (Ephesians 2:10).

In Psalms 32:8 and 33:18 God tells us:

> I will instruct thee and teach thee in the way which thou shalt go: I will guide thee with mine eye.

> Behold, the eye of the Lord is upon them that fear him, upon them that hope in his mercy.

God knew you before He formed you in your mother's belly; He knew you even before you came forth out of your mother's womb (Jeremiah 1:5). God loves you and wants His best for you, and it is yours for the taking. He has given you His Word: "Thus saith the Lord, thy Redeemer, the Holy One of Israel; I am the Lord thy God which teacheth thee to profit, which leadeth thee by the way that thou shouldest go" (Isaiah 48:17). God uses the Holy Spirit to teach you to profit and to lead you into all truth. But you must first take the time to get to know the Holy Spirit on an intimate basis and develop your spirit so that you recognize His voice. You must take advantage of the present opportunities and make sure that you follow your inward witness from now on.

God dwells in us, and that is where He is going to speak to us—in our hearts or our spirits. Our spirits pick things up from the Holy Spirit, and then He passes them on to our minds by an inward intuition.

The No. 1 way God speaks to us is through that inward witness, but He also uses an inward voice. In writing this book I hear that inward voice dictating the words to me, and I only have to write them out. But as I reread the text, I depend on that inward witness to show me any mistakes that I have made.

Your inward man has a voice just as your outward man has a voice. The voice of your inward man is called your conscience, but I have also heard it called intuition, inner guidance, or that still, small voice. Don't let it be confused with the voice of the Holy Spirit speaking to you, because when the

Holy Spirit talks, His voice is more bold and authoritative and with a little practice you will easily be able to tell the difference. (Romans 9:1)

Paul in Acts 23:1 said: "I have lived in all good conscience before God until this day." He was simply telling us that he always obeyed what his spirit was telling him or what he got right down on the inside of him.

It is your choice, you can choose to do things God's way or you can continue doing things the world's way. When you have the life and nature of God in you, your conscience will not permit you to do just anything that you want to do. When you are living that Christian life, you have the Spirit of God living and abiding in your spirit, and you are allowing it to lead you and guide you.

This should make it easy for you to understand why many people do the things that they do. The person who has never been born again cannot follow the voice of his spirit, or conscience, because his unregenerate spirit has the nature of the devil in it. His conscience simply permits him to do anything that he wants.

If you are a Christian, the Holy Spirit will not condemn you, but as your comforter, He will show you the way out. He is your helper; He's not there to condemn you. I John 3:20–21 (AMP) explains this:

> Whenever our hearts in [tormenting] self-accusation make us feel guilty and condemn us. [For we are in God's hands.] For He is above and greater than our consciences (our hearts), and He knows (perceives and understands) everything [nothing is hidden from Him].
>
> And beloved, if our consciences (our hearts) do not accuse us [if they do not make us feel guilty and condemn us], we have confidence (complete assurance and boldness) before God.

Is it God that condemns you? No, it is God that justified you—made you upright and in right standing with God—by his grace through the redemption that is in Christ Jesus (Romans 3:24). It is your conscience, the voice of your spirit that condemns you when you do something wrong. Your spirit knows it the very moment you have done something wrong, and it is up to you to obey it instantly.

You must keep a clear conscience, because it is your conscience, the voice of your spirit, that relates to your mind what the Spirit of God is saying to you down inside. If you don't keep a tender conscience, spiritual things will not be clear to you.

I John 1:9 tells us "If we confess our sins, he is faithful and just to forgive us our sins and to cleanse us from all unrighteousness." When you miss it, just say, "Lord, forgive me. I have missed it." And if you have offended someone, ask for their forgiveness also.

When you let your spirit dominate you, God will enlighten you through your spirit. But you must let the new man, that new creature found in II Corinthians 5:17 that has been reborn and lives on the inside be the dominant one. You must walk by your spirit and not let your body dominate you because it will want to keep doing the same old things that it has been doing. Remember:

> There is therefore now no condemnation to them which are in Christ Jesus, who walk not after the flesh, but after the spirit. (Romans 8:1)

> … walk in the spirit, and ye shall not fulfill the lust of the flesh. (Galatians 5:16)

Your conscience is the voice of your human spirit. Your reason is the voice of your soul, or your mind. And your feelings are the voice of your body.

The Holy Spirit does not bear witness with our reasoning, and it does not bear witness with our feelings, but it bears witness with our spirits. It is something that you sense spiritually, because it is not a feeling. Remember, God is a spirit, and He deals with us in the spiritual realm, not the physical realm.

If you go by your feelings, you'll get yourself into trouble. The devil is a flesh devil, and he works by manipulating your feelings. That is why so many people are up one day and down the next. They are listening to their feelings and acting on it. Those people are always trying to get spiritual answers from the physical, and it just doesn't work that way. It is when you do things God's way that He causes you to triumph in Christ (II Corinthians 2:14).

Faith and hope have nothing to do with your feelings; they are based on what God's Word says and nothing else. If you feel down and depressed, that is the time to just open your mouth and start praising God for who He is and what He is doing in your life. Use the following as an example and continue on:

Dear Lord, I'm so glad I'm a born-again, spirit-filled, holy, righteous, justified son of God. I'm so glad that I have been born again. I am a new creation in Christ Jesus; old things are passed away, behold all things become new. My inward man is a new man, and I am filled with the Holy Spirit. I present my body to You for it is the temple of the Living God. You, Lord, dwell in me, and Your life permeates my spirit, soul, and body so that I am filled with the fullness of God daily, and I am complete in Him. I just want to thank you for it, Lord. In Jesus' Name.

When you do that, you are stirring up the gift of God that is in you by putting yourself in remembrance of whom and what you are in Christ (II Timothy 1:6; II Peter 1:13).

Smith Wigglesworth once wrote,

I am not moved by what I feel.
I am not moved by what I see.
I am moved only by what I believe.
I can't understand God by my feelings.
I can't understand the Lord Jesus Christ by my feelings.
I understand God by what the Word says about Him.
I understand the Lord Jesus Christ by what the Word says about Him.
He is everything the Word says He is.

You will never be able to understand yourself by your feelings. Instead, you must understand yourself as a born-again, spirit-filled, holy, righteous, justified Christian by what the Word of God says about you. When you confess what the Word of God says about you, your confidence in Him and your confidence in yourself will grow, and you will soon see yourself walking by faith and not by sight (II Corinthians 5:7).

For more faith building confessions of faith, check out the last chapter of this book. Remember to always, "Thank [God] in everything [no matter what the circumstances may be, be thankful and give thanks], for this is the will of God for you [who are] in Christ Jesus [the Revealer and Mediator of that will]" (I Thessalonians 5:18) AMP.

Did you notice that it says to give thanks to God in everything and not for everything? As you make a positive confession of faith you are making a demand on your covenant with God and you are requiring Him to act on your behalf according to Isaiah 45:11, "...and concerning the work of my hands command ye me."

As an example I am going to use Isaiah 53:5. "But he was wounded for our transgressions; he was bruised for our iniquities: the chastisement of our peace was upon him; and with his stripes we are healed." Notice the last three words, "...we are healed."

Next, look at Matthew 8:17, "That it might be fulfilled which was spoken by Esaias the prophet, saying, Himself took our infirmities, and bare our sicknesses." And last, look at I Peter 2:24, "Who his own self bare our sins in his own body on the tree, that we, being dead to sins, should live unto righteousness: by whose stripes ye were healed."

Did you notice those last three words? Ye were healed. It doesn't say that you might be healed or you will be healed, it says you were healed.

As such, the next time that you don't feel all that well; your confession should be based not on how you look or feel, but on what God has already done in your life.

You give God the thanks for healing you. You refuse to allow that what is not from God to be in or on your body. You have a right to demand that your body be in perfect chemical balance and that every organ of your body perform a perfect work for you are a temple of the Holy Ghost and you have a right to demand your body to be healed and made whole on the basis of God's holy Word, "…by whose stripes ye were healed," in Jesus' Name.

By your words, you either allow God or the devil to work in your life. As I have said before, the choice is yours! "For by your words you will be justified and acquitted, and by your words you will be condemned and sentenced" (Matthew 12:37 AMP).

Confess: I will do what I was designed to do; I will fellowship with God and I will give Him great pleasure by walking in faith because the Word says that without faith it is impossible to please God (Hebrews 11:6). I will walk in faith and I will not allow myself to be dominated by sin, sickness, fear, and doubt or anything else that is of the devil. I choose to walk in love with God.

3

IN HIM—IN CHRIST

With this in view we constantly pray for you, that our God may deem and count you worthy of [your] calling and [His] every gracious purpose of goodness, and with power may complete in [your] every particular work of faith (faith, which is that leaning of the whole human personality on God in absolute trust and confidence in His power, wisdom, and goodness).

Thus may the name of the Lord Jesus Christ be glorified and become more glorious through and in you, and may you [also be glorified] in Him according to the grace (favor and blessing) of our God and the Lord Jesus Christ (the Messiah, the Anointed One). (I Thessalonians 1:11–12 AMP)

To know who you are "In Him, In Christ" is to know how much God loves you. If you do not understand these terms, you will never have proper insight concerning the truth that your acceptance by God is based on Jesus' performance, not yours. When Jesus died on the cross, you died with Him. When He was buried, you were buried with Him. When He was resurrected, you were resurrected with Him. That is the way God chose to see all of us who sincerely believe in Jesus as our substitutionary sacrifice and the payment for all of our sins. That is what it means to be in Him. When you know who you are in Him, your behavior will change, and you will progressively behave more and more in the ways that are Christlike, which is how Jesus acted while He was here on the earth (II Corinthians 5:15; Romans 6:4; Colossians 2:12; II Corinthians 5:18–19 AMP; Colossians 2:9–14 AMP)

Your focus should be on living your life in Christ. When you make the decision to live in Christ and for Christ, you will experience a change in your lifestyle—one that is based on the Christian principles found in the Word of God. The Word of God is designed to shape your principles, and they will rule your thoughts and shape your opinions, ideas, doctrines, and creeds. They will actually propel you in a certain direction in life each and every day."

For there is one God, and one mediator between God and men, the man Christ Jesus" (I Timothy 2:5).

Man's spiritual condition after the fall of Adam demanded an incarnation, because man had become spiritually dead with no avenue of approach to God. The incarnation of deity with humanity provided one who could stand as man's mediator. Equal with God on one hand and united with man on the other, this one could assume the obligations of man's treason and satisfy the claims of justice, thereby bridging the gap between God and man.

God created man in His own image (Genesis 1:27) just a little lower than Himself (Psalms 8:5–6 AMP). In fact, man was created so nearly like God that it was possible for God and man to become united for eternity in one individual. (When Christ became a man and took on a physical body in the incarnation, He did so for eternity. Therefore, there is a God-man in heaven today at the Father's right hand as a result of the incarnation.) That is what made it possible for God and man to become united!

God now dwells in us and is imparting His life and nature into our spirits. That is what takes place at the new birth where we become new creatures in Christ. Spiritual death was eradicated from our spirits, old things were passed away, and God gave us His life (Colossians 2:9–14 AMP).

II Corinthians 5:17 says, "Therefore if any man be *in Christ*, he is a new creature; old things are passed away; behold all things are become new." As a new believer, you are a new creature, a new creation in Christ Jesus living in an old, unresurrected body. You are still in the flesh, having an unsurrendered soul, and a born-again spirit indwelt by the Spirit of God. That old nature, your unsurrendered soul will be the root of most of your problems.

As your new spiritual nature begins to grow in you, the trouble begins. Your old nature will become sharply aware that something has suddenly appeared on the scene that could be totally disastrous to the free rein it has held on your life, and it will respond in kind.

God, in His infinite wisdom, has made provision for us to walk into renewal and restoration right here on this earth while we are still in our mortal bodies. Titus 3:5 (NIV) says, "He saved us, not because of any righteous things we had done, but because of his mercy. He saved us through the washing of rebirth and renewal by the Holy Spirit."

Many people have experienced the new birth in Christ Jesus but still hold on tightly to their old ways because they have never been taught how to be led by their spirits (Romans 8:14). They have neither learned how to "… put off the old man with his deeds; And have put on the new man, which is renewed in knowledge after the image of him that created him," (Colossians 3:9–10) nor how to present their bodies to God knowing that they are the temple of the Holy Ghost (I Corinthians 6:19). They don't know that God dwells in them and that His life permeates their spirits, souls, and bodies so that they are filled with the fullness of God daily (Romans 12:1–2; John 14:20).

It is vitally important for all of us to know and understand just how cleansing the blood of Jesus really is. When Jesus shed His blood for the sins of the world, it was extremely powerful and unique. It made a way for each one of us to get rid of his old, sinful ways and all of the crap that is associated with it and start over as a brand new creature in Christ—fresh and holy, blameless before God.

You are not an old sinner saved by grace but a new creation created in Christ Jesus. Your past has been wiped totally clean by the blood of Jesus, and His righteousness has made you pure before God! (II Corinthians 5:17).

There were several new features planted into that new you, including the love of God, joy, and generosity. You became free from unforgiveness and strife, and you are now expected to forgive others as Christ has forgiven you for the love of God is now being shed abroad in your heart by the Holy Ghost (Matthew 6:12; Romans 5:5).

We have all received God's covenant rights that He has for His children, and these include being able to override Satan and break loose from his bondages. Jesus said in John 14:12, "He that believeth on me, the works that I do shall he do also; and greater works than these shall he do; because I go unto my Father." God has given us an assignment, and He has made provision for us to provide us with everything that we need to complete the task.

Colossians 2:9–15 details just what Jesus accomplished in providing for us all that we need to carry out the assignment that the Father has for us.

> For in him dwelleth all the fullness of the Godhead bodily.
>
> And ye are complete in him, which is the head of all principality and power:
>
> In whom also ye are circumcised with the circumcision made without hands, in putting off the body of the sins of the flesh by the circumcision of Christ:

> Buried with him in baptism, wherein also ye are risen with him through the faith of the operation of God, who hath raised him from the dead.
>
> And you, being dead in your sins and the uncircumcision of your flesh, hath he quickened together with him, having forgiven you all trespasses;
>
> Blotting out the handwriting of ordinances that was against us, which was contrary to us, and took it out of the way, nailing it to his cross;
>
> And having spoiled principalities and powers, he made a shew of them openly, triumphing over them in it. (I John 3:8)

Notice the words in Colossians 2:12, "through the faith of the operation of God." Jesus was quickened or made alive by the faith of the operation of God, and we were made alive at the same time (Galatians 2:20; Romans 8:11; Colossians 2:9–10).

Notice it was God who raised Jesus from the dead (Romans 8:11). It was God who gave Jesus a Name above every name (Philippians 2:9). It was God who blotted out "the handwriting of ordinances" against us, took it out of the way, and nailed it to His cross (Colossians 2:14). It was God who stripped the powers of darkness, those principalities and powers, of their authority and handed it to the Son (Colossians 2:15). And it was God who quickened us "together with Him" (Ephesians 2:5).

In the mind of God, legally speaking, it was when Jesus was quickened and made alive that you were re-created in him. "For we are his workmanship, created in Christ Jesus unto good works" (Ephesians 2:10)

This fact of your re-creation needs to become a reality in your life: that when you were born again, you were virtually made a new creature, raised with Christ, quickened with Him, and seated with Him at the right hand of the Father! (II Corinthians 5:17; Ephesians 2:4–6).

This is God's will for your life—that you know and understand just who and what you are in Christ Jesus and what He has called you to do. But you will have to make the choice to answer the call on your life here on the earth and get yourself into alignment and agreement with God's will in heaven. God will never force you to do anything, but He will help you. The will of God will never take you where His grace will not keep and support you.

Philippians 2:13 (AMP) tells us that "[Not in your own strength] for it is God Who is all the while effectually at work in you [energizing and creating in you the power and desire], both to will and to work for His good pleasure and satisfaction and delight."

Any limitations that you will encounter in your walk with God will be self-imposed, because nothing is impossible with God and "All things are possible to him that believeth" (Mark 9:23; Ephesians 6:10; Philippians 4:13).

Colossians 1:18 tells us that "… he is the head of the body, the church: who is the beginning, the firstborn from the dead; that in all things he might have the preeminence."

You need to recognize that Jesus is the Head of the Church, and as the head, He is wholly dependent upon its body for carrying out its plans. That is why it is so important for you to know and understand that you are seated with Christ in heavenly places and that you have authority over Satan's power. If this authority is ever exercised, it will have to be exercised through the body, because the Head is powerless without the body.

The ministry work that God wants to accomplish through His Son in this world will be carried out through the body of Christ, and that is you and me. And we, as the body of Christ, have the same authority that the head has.

In Matthew 28:18–19 (AMP), Jesus said, "All authority (all power of rule) in heaven and on earth has been given to me. Go then …"

Who is to go and do? You, the body!

The authority on earth that is invested in the Name of Jesus Christ and was obtained by Him through His overcoming Satan at the cross was delegated by Jesus Christ to the Church. Jesus spoke these words in Matthew 28 after His death on the cross, after His burial, after His defeat of Satan in hell, after His resurrection, and after His ascension with His own blood to the heavenly Holy of Holies but just before His ascension to be seated at the right hand of the Father.

Jesus said that all authority in Heaven and on earth is given to Him. Then He immediately transferred this authority on earth to His Church, saying, "Go ye therefore …" (Matthew 28:19).

The devil doesn't want you to know who you are in Christ and that Jesus is alive in you. He doesn't want you to know that God has given you the power of attorney to use the Name of Jesus, because that Name has authority in this earth. He doesn't want you to know that the use of that name is not a matter of faith, but it is a matter of assuming your legal rights in Christ, taking your place as a son of God, and using what belongs to you! (John 1:12).

Hosea 4:6 says that "my people are destroyed for lack of knowledge." And what don't they know? They don't know that faith is the doorway to abundance. It is the key to unlimited treasure. Its laws of operation are sure, steadfast, and as unchanging as Jesus Himself. In giving Himself to us, He has given us His faith. Not just a portion of it but all of it. As such, He did not give us only a portion of Himself but everything that He has and is, has been given to us in full measure.

You must spend time meditating these verses over and over until you know this for sure. "According as his divine power hath given unto us all things that pertain unto life and godliness through the knowledge of him that hath called us to glory and virtue" (II Peter 1:3–4).

God has given to us "... all things that pertain unto life and godliness through the knowledge of him...." These things belong to you, but just like Abraham, you must get yourself to the point where you are "... fully persuaded that, what he had promised, he was able also to perform" (Romans 4:17–21). This is God's method of calling things that are not as though they were until they are. God loves you that much.

The devil simply doesn't like for us to enter into and mess around in his domain. He has been used to exercising authority and ruling over people's lives with no interference, so you should expect him to concentrate his forces against you when you come into these mighty truths. I don't believe that there is anything that upsets the devil more than when someone gets a revelation of the truth of the authority that they have as a believer and starts to walk in it (Matthew 28:18; Luke 10:19).

Always remember that "... greater is he that is in you, that he that is in the world" (I John 4:4). Christ in you is greater than all of those principalities and powers, rulers of the darkness of this world and against spiritual wickedness in high places. (Ephesians 6:12)

The safest place to be is to be is to be seated with Christ in heavenly places, far above all principality, power, might, and dominion. And if you will abide steadfastly by faith in this place, you cannot be touched by the devil and his crowd. That is why it is so important to take your seat in the heavenly places with Christ and keep it (Ephesians 1:20–21).

Notice how Jesus handled the devil in Matthew 4:4–7. He simply told the devil that "It is written" and then simply quoted the appropriate scripture to him. That is how one acts who is seated with Christ in heavenly places.

The morning that Jesus came out of the tomb two men in shining garments spoke to the women who had come to place spices and ointments on His body and said, "Why seek ye the living among the dead? He is not here, but is risen" (Luke 24:5–6). Don't look for Jesus among the dead, lifeless religions of the world. Look for Him where the action is: among born-again, spirit-filled saints who are out saving the lost, healing the sick, and raising the dead.

Jesus is alive, and His Word is alive. Hebrews 4:12 (AMP) says, "For the Word that God speaks is alive and full of power [making it active, operative, energizing, and effective]; it is sharper than any two-edged sword, penetrating to the dividing line of the breath of life (soul) and [the immortal] spirit, and of joints and marrow [of the deepest parts of our nature], exposing and sifting and analyzing and judging the very thoughts and purposes of the heart."

Two-edged, from the Greek *distomos*, is a compound of the word *di*, meaning "two," and the word *stomos*, which is the Greek word for "one's mouth." Now, with the two words connected, we have one word, *distomos*, which describes something or someone that is "two-mouthed." The Bible is comparing the Word of God to a "two-edged sword" or, literally, a "two-mouthed sword"!

The Word of God is like a sword that has two edges, cutting both ways and doing terrible damage to an aggressor. Ephesians 6:17 calls it "the sword of the Spirit," which is simply the Word of God. The word *word* is from the Greek *rhema*, which describes "something that is spoken clearly, vividly, in unmistakable terms and undeniable language." And it carries the idea of a "quickened word."

If you have ever been praying about a situation and suddenly a Bible verse popped up on the inside of your heart, you have received a *rhema* word that came right out of the mouth of God. It was dropped into your spirit for you to stand on and claim for your situation. That Word of God is so sharp that it is able to cut right through your intellect and your natural logic and lodge itself deep within your heart.

When this happens, it is important for you to spend quality time meditating on that *rhema* word so that it can release its power on the inside of you. And when you do, it will grow, and you will soon have a desire to speak out those words of power and authority. When you do, they will contain the power to drive back the forces of hell that have been marshaled against you.

First, that word came out of the mouth of God. Second, it came out of your mouth, and when it came out of your mouth, it became a sharp, two-edged," or literally, a "two-mouthed," sword. The one edge of the sword came into existence initially when the Word proceeded out of God's mouth, and the second edge was added when the Word of God proceeded out of your mouth. If you fail to meditate that rhema word and allow it to build up in your spirit before releasing it, it will simply lay dormant in your heart and never become the second edge of that two-edged sword that God had designed it to be.

When you do your part and rise up and begin to speak forth that word, something happens in the realm of the Spirit. The moment that Word of God comes out of your mouth and you make Jesus Christ the High Priest of your confession, a second edge is added to the blade. At that moment you and God come into agreement, and that agreement releases His mighty power into the situation that you are praying about (Amos 3:3; Matthew 18:19).

For you to be strong in faith, the first thing that you must get settled on is the integrity of the Word of God. You must not have any doubt that the Bible is exactly what it declares itself to be: the Word of God or God speaking directly to you as a revelation from Him to you. You must also be fully persuaded that what God has promised you he is able also to perform (Romans 4:21).

I Peter 1:23 tells you that you were "... born again, not of corruptible seed, but of incorruptible, by the word of God, which liveth and abideth for ever. We were brought forth from death in trespass and sin by the very same Word of His power—the Word of God which lives and abides forever!"

And in Ephesians 2:5–6 (AMP) we are told that:

> Even when we were dead (slain) by [our own] shortcomings and trespasses, He made us alive together in fellowship and in union with Christ; [He gave us the very life of Christ Himself, the same new life with which He quickened Him, for] it is by grace (His favor and mercy which you did not deserve) that you are saved (delivered from judgment and made partakers of Christ's salvation).
>
> And He raised us up together with Him and made us sit down together [giving us joint seating with Him] in the heavenly sphere [by virtue of our being] in Christ Jesus (the Messiah, the Anointed One).

We are just as alive as He is. His life is living in us now. Not after we get to heaven, but right now! This is what the Holy Spirit is telling us in I John 4:17: "... as he is, so are we in this world."

Not later, but now! We are the sons of the Living God (John 1:12). And I John 5:1 tells us that "Whosoever believeth that Jesus is the Christ is Born of God..." And verse 4 tells that: "For whatsoever is born of God overcometh the world: and this is the victory that overcometh the world, even our faith."

Jesus is alive. His Word is alive. We are alive. That means His faith, which has become our faith, is alive. In fact, His faith is in His Word, according to Romans 10:17. His faith is a living force. His faith, His hope, His love—all three are alive in us ready to do the same works that they did when He was here on the earth. And in John 14:12, Jesus said, "... He that believeth on me, the works that I do shall he do also; and greater works than these shall he do; because I go unto my Father."

The world is looking for people who believe God's Word and are willing to share it with others. We were born into this world for that purpose for this time, and His Glory is being manifested for that very purpose.

God has equipped us with His Word, which is his wisdom and knowledge. Colossians 2:10 tells us that we are complete in Him. We don't need anything more!

In Colossians 2:3 (AMP) we see that "In Him all the treasures of [divine] wisdom (comprehensive insight into the ways and purpose of God) and [all the riches of spiritual] knowledge and enlightenment are stored up and lie hidden." All of the treasures of wisdom and knowledge are hidden in Him, and that is where we are" in Him. So all of that wisdom and knowledge is in us!

I would suggest that you read and meditate all of the verses that pertain to phrases such as – In Him, in whom, in Christ etc.

Colossians 2:9–10 tells us that:

> For *in Him* dwelleth all the fullness of the Godhead bodily.
> And *you are complete in Him*, which is the head of all principality and power.

You and I have the same access to use the faith of God as Jesus does. After all, He is as much your Father as He is Jesus' Father. You are as much His child as Jesus is. Mark 9:23 says that "… all things are possible to him that believeth."

Paul went so far in Galatians 2:20 (AMP) to say, "I have been crucified with Christ [in Him I have shared His crucifixion]; it is no longer I who live, but Christ (the Messiah) liveth in me; and the life I now live in the body I live by faith in (by adherence to and reliance on and complete trust in) the Son of God, Who loved me and gave Himself up for me."

Acts 10:34 tells us "that God is no respecter of persons" and that His presence is available to every believer. Ignorance works for the enemy, the devil, because it gives him freedom to pursue and conquer without being noticed.

You and I need to have confidence in whom we are in Christ, for "greater is he that is in you, than he that is in the world" (I John 4:4).

Confess: Greater is the Christ, The Anointed one and His Anointing (that burden-removing, yoke-destroying power of God that is in me) than he who is in the world. This includes all principalities, powers, rulers of the darkness, of this world, and spiritual wickedness in high places. That same power that raised Jesus from the dead now lives on the inside of me and is at my disposal twenty-four hours a day, seven days a week allowing me to do the same works that Jesus did! (Ephesians 6:12; I John 5:4; John 14:12).

The day you received Jesus into your life as your Lord and personal savior, the Holy Ghost came on the inside of you. He is now ready to break out in your mouth, on your hands, and in your mind and give you wisdom, knowledge, and understanding. He is ready to come up on you and give you the confidence to declare that Jesus is anointed and so am I (I Corinthians 6:19).

The ball is in your court. It is up to you to step up and step out and start acting like a born-again child of God is suppose to act. God expects you to act just like Jesus did when he walked here on this earth, when He exercised His authority as The Father directed Him (John 5:19, 30; 8:28).

Note: Take extra time and read and meditate John 5:19–47; 8:28–29; 17. The relationship that Jesus has with the Father is the same one that He wishes to have with you, and you being in Christ is what has given you the right to experience it. When you step out in faith as God gives you direction, you have every right to expect God to act on your behalf just as He did for Jesus. It is the Father that does the work (John 6:29) not you.

As an example, Mark 16:18 tells us that when "they (the believer) shall lay hands on the sick, and they shall recover." Your responsibility is to lay your hands on the sick, and it is God's responsibility to cause them to recover.

4

THE KEY OF FAITH

> Now Faith is the assurance (the confirmation, the title deed)
> of the things [we] hope for, being the proof of things [we] do
> not see and the conviction of their reality [faith perceiving as
> real fact what is not revealed to the senses]. (Hebrews 11:1
> AMP)

Faith comes from the Greek work *pistis*, which means conviction of the
truth of anything. When it relates to God, *pistis* is the conviction that God
exists and is the creator and ruler of all things, the provider and bestower of
eternal salvation through Jesus Christ.

Faith is simply choosing to believe God and His Word above everything
else and acting on it. As a born-again son of God, you choose to believe that
Jesus is the first begotten Son of God (Revelation 1:5) and that He came to
save those who were lost. You made a confession of faith based on that belief.
You made a choice to believe God and you made a confession of faith based
on what you heard even though you couldn't see, hear, taste, or feel anything,
because faith is not mental assent or mental agreement. It is when you act
on God's Word that it becomes a reality, because it is your faith that puts the
power of God to work.

Faith confessions create realities. As far as God is concerned, everything
you have or are in Christ is so. He has done it. Everything that the Bible
says is yours, and it is yours legally. The Bible is a legal document, sealed
by the blood of Jesus. You are an heir of God and a joint-heir with Christ
according to the promise (Romans 8:17; Galatians 4:7). Everything that the
Bible promises you is yours. However, it is your believing it in your heart and
your confessing it with your mouth that makes it a reality to you. God wants

you to enjoy and know the reality of what He has provided for you, and His Word tells you how to do it.

As God reveals Himself to us through the scripture by a revelation of His Name, we can know him and become more like Him. Remember to keep your focus on the Word. Whatever has your focus affects your faith, and whatever affects your faith affects your harvest.

Satan knows that empty heads are much easier to deceive. That's why he loves it when he finds a believer who has made no effort to fill his or her mind with the truth from the Word of God. He loves to make a playground out of people's minds and imaginations. He delights in filling their perceptions and senses with illusions that captivate them, paralyze them, and ultimately destroy them. He knows it when he has found another empty head just waiting for him to come along and fill it with his lies and deceit.

You must decide who or what is going to control your mind—God and His Word or the enemy and his lies. Your mind is going to be filled with something, so you may as well choose the right thing to fill it with. To avoid falling victim to the devil's attacks, you must make a spiritual decision to take charge of every thought that enters your mind. Your choice in the matter will determine your success or your failure in life, so make sure you choose wisely!

THE APOSTLE AND HIGH PRIEST OF OUR PROFESSION

Jesus is the Apostle and High Priest of your confession, and He is responsible to cause your confession of faith to come to pass. Jesus put His ministry under faith's command, and every time you make a decision that is in line with God's Word and act upon it, He is under your command to do it. God is love, and love puts itself at faith's command (Isaiah 45:11).

Hebrews 3:1 tells us that Jesus Christ is "… the Apostle and High Priest of our profession." The word *profession* can also be translated *confession*, and it refers to the words that we speak. Its literal translation is "to say the same thing." Jesus now sits at the right hand of Almighty God, and it is one of His duties to cause or bring to pass the words that we speak when we make confessions of faith based on the Word of God.

The Word of God is living, breathing, and moving. It's pulsating with the energy of God, but it requires your faith to move it from the page to the present. That's how you get results when you act in faith. Faith comes by hearing the Word of God, and faith grows by exercising it. Faith and experience turns your hope into manifested reality. No matter what the problem is, God's Word has something to say about it. God's Word has the answer. It is your job to find out what the Word says and act like it's true.

The Word of God is living and powerful, and in its treasure, you will find eternal life and your every need met in abundance. If you will dare to trust this wonderful Lord of life, you will find in Him everything that you need.

The Holy Spirit, who inspired the Word of God, is called the Spirit of truth, (John 14:17, 15:26, 16:13; I John 4:6), and if you will receive and implement with meekness the engrafted Word, faith will spring up in your heart—faith in the sacrifice of Calvary, faith in the shed blood of Jesus, faith in the fact that Jesus took our weaknesses upon Himself, faith that He has borne our sicknesses and carried our pains, and faith that He is in your life today (Isaiah 53:4–5; I Peter 2:24).

Each one of us has been given a measure of faith when we asked Jesus into our lives as our Lord and Savior (Romans 12:3). And it is enough faith to make sure that we are covered for any event that may come along in our new life in Christ (Romans 10:9–10). We all received that same measure of faith, the Holy Spirit and the power that will allow us to make changes in our lives as we take the time and the effort to hear the Word of God and apply and protect that measure of faith. Most new Christians simply don't know this and that measure of faith is never activated or put into use in their lives.

There are two things that you never have to pray for: faith and power. Faith comes by hearing the Word of God, not by reading what others think the Word of God means or says. If you need more faith, just spend more time reading and listening to the Word of God (Romans 10:17).

Power comes because faith is power, and power is authority. Remember, Romans 1:16 tells us that "The Gospel is the power of God unto salvation." The Greek and Hebrew word *salvation* implies the idea of material and temporal deliverance from danger and apprehension, preservation, pardon, restoration, healing wholeness, and soundness.

In Matthew 28:18, Jesus said, "All power is given unto me." And in John 17:23, we see where Jesus was praying to the Father: "I in them, and thou in me."

You are one with the Father, and in I Corinthians 3:16, you are told that "you are the temple of God, and the Spirit of God lives in you."

I Corinthians 6:19 instructs you to "Know ye not that your body is the temple of the Holy Ghost." And II Corinthians 6:16 tells you that "ye are the temple of the living God." And in Acts 1:8 Jesus said that "You will receive power after that the Holy Ghost is come upon you."

Believing that the Holy Ghost and God's power has come upon you is what allows you to be a partaker of the divine nature of God through His great and precious promises (II Peter 1:3–4).

How did Jesus get that power? In Acts 10:38, we see where "God anointed Jesus with the Holy Ghost and with power." In John 17:21, Jesus asked the Father "that we would be one with Him as He is one with the Father." In Galatians 2:20, Paul said that it wasn't he that lived but Christ (the Anointed One and his anointing) that lives in him. The life that Paul was living was by the faith of the Son of God who loved him and gave Himself for him. Finally, in Colossians 2:10, we are told that "we are complete in Him," complete meaning we have no part lacking.

When you invited Jesus Christ into your life as your Lord and Savior, you became a new creation in Christ Jesus—all of the old things are passed away, and all things have become new. Your spirit was re-created in Christ Jesus. He moved in, and you received all of the power that God possesses. I John 5:4 tells us that "whosoever is born of God overcometh the world."

Why? Because it is simply not possible for us to overcome the world if we don't have the God given power to do so (Romans 10:9–10; Matthew 28:18; II Corinthians 5:17). You can have a life of power by learning how to release your faith, but your faith will not work if you do not obey God's commandment to walk in love (Matthew 22:37–39; Mark 12:30–31; I John 5:3).

Mark 16:17 tells us that "These signs shall follow them that believe." What is it to believe? It is to have such confidence in what the Lord said that we would take Him at His word and act upon it simply because He said it.

If you can believe that God "hath given you all things that pertain unto life and godliness, and get hold of the exceeding great and precious promises of God, His power will constantly be visible on your life (II Peter 1:3–4).

There is something about believing in God and exercising your faith that makes Him willing to pass over many just to anoint you with His power. God's grace will always turn out to meet you right where you are if you will only dare to believe His Word. God's power working in you will bring forth a divine order that can never be surpassed by anything in this world, because a person filled with the Holy Ghost has the ability to be extraordinary.

Ephesians 6:10 instructs us to "… be strong in the Lord and the power of His might" (II Corinthians 10:3). You become strong in the Lord by exercising your faith. The word *strong* as used here is the Greek word *endunamao,* a compound of the words *en* and *dunamis.* The word *en* means "in," and the word *dunamis* means "explosive strength, ability, and power." It's where the word *dynamite* comes from.

The word *endunamao* presents the picture of an explosive power that is being deposited into some type of container, vessel, or other form of receptacle.

So the very nature of this word *indunamao* means that there is a necessity for there to be some type of a receiver for this power to be deposited into.

Genesis 1:26 tells us that we have been made in the God class, which indicates that we are specially designed by God to be the receptacles of divine power. By being instructed in Ephesians 6:10 to "be strong in the Lord and the power of His might," we are being directed to receive a supernatural, strengthening, internal deposit of God's power into your inner man. Notice that God is the giver, and we are the receptacles into which this power is to be deposited.

For your faith to work, you need to be walking in God's love by not being selfish or stingy but instead by being willing and excited about sharing the blessing of God with others in order to promote God's glory and the good of your fellow man (Galatians 3:14; I John 4:12).

Hebrews 11:1 tells us "Now faith is." Faith is the principal substance of the Word of God that allows God to work in our lives. Faith starts where the will of God stops. Faith always says what the Word of God says and brings to pass the things that we are hoping for. Your faith comes by hearing the Word of God, and your faith is activated by speaking out and acting on those words that you have heard. Faith never fails to obtain its desired goal. Faith is a now thing. It's not a maybe thing or a you never know what God might or might not be going to do thing. It contains the substance to create a future.

"Now faith is the substance." There is a substance to faith because "Faith is the substance of things hoped for, the evidence of things not seen." But faith is not in the realm of things that are seen.

Did you ever wonder why? If you cannot see it, then neither can the devil! The evidence of faith is not seen because the devil is not a faith devil but a flesh devil. Have you ever noticed that the devil has never tempted you in the spiritual realm? He has never tempted you to do anything that is in the will of God, such as obeying the laws of God concerning loving God and your neighbor as yourself, tithing, giving, or anything that is of a spiritual concept. He will only tempt you in the flesh, and that is why we are directed to crucify our flesh daily so that we will not fulfill the lust of the flesh.

The most important words on faith in the Bible are found in the book of Mark. Starting with Mark 11:22 where He demonstrated the God-kind of faith for us in verse 14 when He simply said to that tree, "No man eat fruit of thee hereafter for ever." Then He told us to have it also:

> And Jesus answering said unto them, Have faith in God.
> [Or have the God kind of faith.]
> For verily I say unto you. That whosoever shall say unto
> this mountain, Be thou removed, and be thou cast into the

sea; and shall not doubt in his heart, but shall believe that those things which he saith shall come to pass; he shall have whatsoever he saith.

Therefore I say unto you, what things soever you desire, when you pray, believe that you receive them and you shall have them

And when you stand praying, forgive, if you have aught against any: that your Father also which is in heaven may forgive you your trespasses.

But if you do not forgive, neither will your Father which is in heaven forgive your trespasses.

That God-kind of faith is one where you believe in your heart that what you are saying with your mouth will come to pass, and God says you will have it. That is the same kind of faith that God used to create this world that we live in. In the beginning He simply believed that what He said would come to pass. He said, "Let the waters under the heaven be gathered together unto one place and let the dry land appear; and it was so" (Genesis 1:9).

God created the earth and all that is on it by simply speaking it into existence. He believed that it would come to pass by calling those things that be not as though they were. Everything that is here with the exception of man came that way (Genesis 2:7; Romans 4:17-22).

Notice in Mark 11:14 Jesus said unto a fig tree: "No man eat fruit of thee hereafter for ever." And in verses 20 – 22 it says that:

> ... in the morning, as they passed by, they saw the fig tree dried up from the roots.
>
> And Peter calling to remembrance saith unto him, Master, behold, the fig tree which thou cursedst is withered away.
>
> And Jesus answering saith unto them, Have faith in God.

Or have the God-kind of faith. This was a demonstration to the Apostles that He had that kind of faith, the same faith that He had used to create the world in the beginning (John 1:10; Hebrews 1:2).

My purpose is to show you that as a born-again believer you have a measure of that "God-kind of faith." This faith comes as part of your righteousness, or your rights and privileges as a son of God. But the limitations to how much faith you have are self-imposed, for nothing is impossible to God (Mark 10:27).

It does not take great faith to believe in something that cannot fail. The Word of God cannot fail, because it is God Himself (John 1:1). The question that you must ask yourself is this: do I believe that God can do His job if I do what He is asking me to do?

Your faith is not just the words that you speak but is also what you believe and what you act upon. It is what is in abundance in your heart that will carry the day for you when you step out and fill your position as an ambassador for God in his Kingdom.

Remember, it is not your ability to please God but God's ability in you, and it is your responsibility to quit trying and to surrender everything to Him. You don't have to prove anything to God by your works; you are simply required to listen to what God is directing you to do. Do it, and allow Him to provide for all your needs as you do it.

Proverbs 3:6 tells us to "In all thy ways acknowledge him, and he shall direct thy path."

To acknowledge from the Greek *yada,* to know by observing and reflecting [thinking] and to know by experiencing.

Confess: Father, because I have set my love upon You. You have shown me my salvation. You have made known to me the mystery of the Gospel of Jesus Christ, which is the power of God unto my salvation (Romans 1:16).

This Gospel is the power of God unto my deliverance, it is the power of God unto my safety, it is the power of God unto my preservation and it is the power of God unto my healing and my health. It is more than enough. (Psalm 91:15-16)

5

THAT MEASURE OF FAITH

Romans 12:3 tells us: "For I say, through the grace given unto me, to every man that is among you, not to think of himself more highly than he ought to think; but to think soberly, according as God hath dealt to every man the measure of faith." Notice that Paul is not talking to everybody in the world but to the believers only, "every man among you." II Thessalonians 3:2 supports this: "… for all (ungodly) men have not faith."

Anybody that confesses that he doesn't have any faith needs to be saved. Saved people have faith, because you can't be saved without it. Ephesians 2:8–10 says, "For by grace are you saved through faith; and that not of yourselves: it is the gift of God. Not of works, least any man should boast. For we are his workmanship, created in Christ Jesus unto good works, which God hath before ordained that we should walk in them."

Simply put, if a person doesn't have faith, he is not saved.! Romans 12:3 tells us that God has dealt to all believers a measure of faith, but most of them either don't know it or recognize it or are not using their faith. Many believers are taking sides against God and against themselves, because they don't know what the Word of God says.

The moment that you received Jesus as your Lord and Savior by faith, God sowed His Spirit and Word into your heart like a seed, and you were spiritually born again by the incorruptible seed of the Word of God (I Peter1:23). And just like a seed of corn always produces corn, and soybeans always produce soybeans, God's seed on the inside of you immediately began to produce God. God's Word is God speaking to you. God and His Word are one, and God says that you do have faith—the same God-kind of faith that created the world. You have a measure of mountain-moving faith that you received as a gift from God (Ephesians 2:8).

You received that measure of faith by hearing the Word of God. Romans 10:17 says that "So then faith cometh by hearing, and hearing by the word of God." In other words, your level of faith is dependent on your Word intake, and your faith level will grow as your understanding of God's Word grows.

When you listen to God's Words, revelations will come, and those revelations will change your life forever. God has exactly what you need spiritually, physically, financially, and in every other facet of your life.

You will find success in anything you do if you will listen to God's words and follow the revelations He gives you. He gives you that revelation or insight so that you can create change in your life and in the world around you. If you are willing to simply listen, that faith will rise up in your heart.

Read the whole tenth chapter of Romans, and you will see that it is talking about salvation and faith to be saved. Notice in verse 8: "The word is nigh thee, even in thy mouth, and in thy heart; that is, the word of faith, which we preach." God's word is called "the word of faith" because it builds faith or causes faith to come to the heart of those that are open to it.

Now in verses 9, 10, 13, and 14 Paul says:

That if thou shalt confess with thy mouth the Lord Jesus, and shalt believe in thine heart that God hath raised him from the dead, thou shalt be saved.
For with the heart man believeth unto righteousness; and with the mouth confession is made unto salvation.

For whosoever shall call upon the name of the Lord shall be saved.
How then shall they call on him in whom they have not believed? And how shall they believe in him of whom they have not heard? And how shall they hear without a preacher?

Notice, you can't believe in something without hearing. "Faith comes by hearing, and hearing by the Word of God." Your faith in God and the things of God comes by hearing the Word of God, and your faith will grow as your understanding of God's Word grows.

Any time that the devil attacks you with doubt about your salvation, just quote verses 9 and 10 back to him and confess: Because I have confessed with my mouth the Lordship of Jesus Christ over my life and I believe in my heart that Almighty God has raised him from the dead, I am a new creature created in Christ Jesus. For with my heart I believe that I have been made the righteousness of God in Christ Jesus and I am now a born-again son of God. (Romans 8:14–15; 10:9–10, II Corinthians 5:17–21)

This is why where you go to church matters. If what you are hearing doesn't build faith in your heart or in your spirit, you shouldn't be going there. Doubt and unbelief are powerful forces, and they have robbed entire churches of the blessings that God intended for them.

Some churches teach the Word but water it down to the point where it is of little or no value to you. Yet others put their own interpretation on it, and that is not going to build your faith either. You should simply ask God where He wants you to go to church.

Let the scriptures interpret themselves; find other scriptures that support and give you a clear picture of what God is trying to teach you. Faith is built or based on fact (God's Word), and unbelief is built or based on theory, and a theory is nothing but a supposition established upon ignorance of the subject under discussion. A theory is not a law, but faith is a law (Romans 3:27).

Have you ever noticed just how many people are willing to believe in a theory over believing a law? Many of our educators are so blinded by the lies of the devil that they don't know what the truth is any more, and instead of finding the truth, they simply teach what is the most popular theory at the present time (II Corinthians 4:4).

Romans 3:27 tells us that faith is a law, and a law is an established principle that will work the same every time for anybody who will get involved in operating and activating those principles.

Nothing just happens; everything happens because of a law. Everything happens for a reason, and everything is governed by laws. There are laws that govern this natural physical realm. There are laws that govern the realm of the spirit, such as the law of the Spirit of life that is in Christ Jesus. The law of the spirit of life will always supersede the laws that govern sin and death (Romans 8:1–2).

II Corinthians 4:13 says, "We having the same spirit of faith, according as it is written, I believed, and therefore have I spoken; we also believe, and therefore speak." "We having"—not trying for it and hoping for it or struggling to get it. No, we have the same spirit of faith.

Confess: I believe it, and therefore, I have spoken; we also believe and therefore speak. The same kind of faith, that same spirit of faith, that same measure of faith that Jesus spoke about in Mark 11:22–24 and Romans 12:3 is in me. I have a measure of that mountain-moving, God-kind of faith that created the world in the beginning, because I am a believer and not a doubter.

Every believer has a measure of the God-kind of faith. God is no respecter of persons (Acts 10:34) and starts every Christian off the same way. He does not give more faith to some and less to others.

It does matter what you do with the faith that God has given to you. Matthew 25:14–30 talks about three men that were given different amounts of talents. The subject here is that it is up to you to do something with that measure of faith or talents that God has given you. That measure of faith can be increased, and you are the one, not God, who can increase it. God has furnished a measure of faith to you and the means by which it can be increased. He has given to each one of us the Word of God whereby your faith can be increased by feeding on or by hearing it or by exercising your faith by putting it into practice (James 2:20; Romans 10:17).

> For the kingdom of heaven is as a man traveling into a far country, who called his own servants, and delivered unto them his goods.
>
> And unto one he gave five talents, to another two, and to another one; to every man according to his several ability, and straightway took his journey.
>
> Then he that had received the five talents went and traded with the same, and made them other five talents.
>
> And likewise he that had received two, he also gained other two.
>
> But he that had received one went and digged in the earth, and hid his lord's money.
>
> After a long time the lord of these servants cometh, and reckoneth with them.
>
> And so he that had received five talents came and brought other five talents, saying, Lord, thou deliveredst unto me five talents; behold, I have gained beside them five talents more.
>
> His lord said unto him, Well done, thou good and faithful servant: thou hast been faithful over a few things. I will make thee ruler over many things: enter thou into the joy of thy lord.
>
> He also that had received two talents came and said, Lord, thou deliveredst unto me two talents: behold, I have gained two other talents beside them.
>
> His lord said unto him, Well done, good and faithful servant; thou hast been faithful over a few things, I will

make thee ruler over many things: enter thou into the joy of thy lord.

Then he which had received the one talent came and said, Lord, I knew thee that thou art an hard man, reaping where thou hast not sown, and gathering where thou hast not strawed:

And I was afraid, and went and hid thy talent in the earth: lo, there thou hast that is thine.

His lord answered and said unto him, Thou wicked and slothful servant, thou knewest that I reap where I sowed not, and gather where I have not strawed.

Thou oughtest therefore to have put my money to the exchangers, and then at my coming I should have received mine own with usury.

Take therefore the talent from him, and give it unto him which hath ten talents.

For unto every one that hath shall be given, and he shall have abundance: but from him that hath not shall be taken away even that which he hath.

And cast ye the unprofitable servant into outer darkness: there shall be weeping and gnashing of teeth. (Matthew 25:14–30)

It is important to notice what the master's response was to the three servants. He considered what the first two servants had achieved to be fantastic, but it was just the beginning. They had proven themselves to be hardworking and capable and had demonstrated responsibility. The master now knew they could be trusted with true riches. Because these two stewards had proven themselves faithful, the master saw a bright future ahead for them. As is always true with God, faithfulness resulted in promotion and great responsibilities. The first two stewards had passed a test on a lower level, and now their master was satisfied to move them upward into even more monumental life assignments.

But when the master came to the third servant and saw that he had accomplished nothing with the money given to him, he told the servant, "... Thou knewest that I reap where I sowed not, and gather where I have not strawed: Thou oughtest therefore to have put my money to the exchangers, and then at my coming I should have received mine own with usury (verses 26–27).

It is obvious that this third servant was not ignorant of the master's expectations. He knew what the master expected from him. In fact, he said "thou knewest," which means the third servant couldn't pretend to be ignorant. He knew that the master expected him to do something significant with what had been Entrusted to him, but he let fear control the situation.

The master would accept no excuses for a lack of increase. It didn't matter how difficult the situation was, how many odds were stacked against his servants, or how impossible it seemed; the master still expected increase. His servants understood that this was his expectation. Thus, the servant who did nothing with his talent found himself in a horrible predicament.

The master called him a wicked and slothful servant (verse 26), and if that wasn't bad enough, in verse 30 he called him "the unprofitable servant."

The words *wicked* and *slothful* are from the Greek *okneros*, which means lazy or idle, and it carries the idea of a person who has a do-nothing attitude; is lethargic, lackadaisical, apathetic, and indifferent; and has a lukewarm attitude toward life. The word *unprofitable* is from the Greek *achreios*, which means useless or a good-for-nothing type of person.

Jesus used this parable to teach those of us who are His followers what He expects of us. The master in the parable vividly illustrates Jesus' sentiments toward people who have great potential but who are too lazy to get up and do something to develop the potential that has been entrusted to them. "And whatsoever ye do in word or deed, do all in the name of the Lord Jesus, giving thanks to God and the Father by him" (Colossians 3:17).

God has filled you with His Spirit (I Corinthians 3:16; II Corinthians 6:16), that same power that raised up Jesus from the dead (Romans 8:11). The anointing, that burden-removing, yoke-destroying power of God, that you have received of Him lives in you (I John 2:27). Jesus has told you that if you believe in Him, the works that He has done, you will do also (John 14:12).

Stop and take a few minutes to ask God how you can be a good and faithful servant to Him, how to perform better at your job, how to give more effort that you've ever given before, and how to help you adjust your attitude so that you can become what God wants you to be at whatever you are asked to do.

The Bible oftentimes uses natural human things to teach us spiritual thoughts. In Matthew 4:4 Jesus said, "Man shall not live by bread alone but by every word that proceedeth out of the mouth of God." Here He is using a natural human term to convey a spiritual thought to us. He is saying to us that bread or food is to the body what the Word of God is to the heart of man.

If you eat food on a regular basis, it will build you up physically, but if you don't get regular exercise, you will just put on the pounds and get flabby. The same is true with faith. You want to feed your faith with God's Word, and you also want to exercise it to keep your faith muscles fit and trim or else you won't be able to do much spiritually. God's word is faith food and is designed to build you up spiritually to enable you to go out and fight the good fight of faith (I Timothy 6:12).

In Romans 8:12, Paul called the message that he preached "The word of faith." He called the Word of God – The word of faith, because this Word of God will cause faith to come into your heart. Romans 10:17 says that faith comes by hearing the Word of God. God's Word will build assurance, confidence, and faith in your spirit. Now it is up to you to exercise it. This measure of faith can be increased by feeding it God's Word and by putting it into practice in your everyday living.

Faith is simply believing in and acting on God's Word. Faith is not mental assent or mental agreement. It is when you act on God's Word that it becomes a reality.

No matter what the problem is, God's Word has something to say about it. God's Word has the answer. Find out what the Word says and act like it's true. Your level of faith is dependent on your Word intake, because the battleground of the mind is where life's most precious victories are won or lost.

The reality of the Word of God is more powerful than your feelings, so you must keep declaring the Word over and over again. Because faith comes by hearing the Word of God and every time that you speak the Word about any given situation, you hear it, and faith comes. If you haven't been maintaining and using your faith, it won't be strong enough to overturn the symptoms that you are feeling, but as you continue to hear the Word and allow your faith to grow, it will get to the point where your faith will dominate the situation and cause you to receive the desired results.

In Mark 4:30–32, Jesus compares the Kingdom of God and His righteousness, God's way of doing and being right (Matthew 6:33 AMP), which is faith, to a mustard seed:

> Whereunto shall we liken the kingdom of God? Or with what comparison shall we compare it?
> It is like a grain of mustard seed, which, when it is sown in the earth, is less than all the seeds that be in the earth:
> But when it is sown, it growth up and becometh greater than all herbs, and shooteth out great branches; so that the fowls of the air may lodge under the shadow of it.

Look at your faith container as a basket that is only partially full, and that partially full basket will not get the job done. That is why you, as believers, must be determined to stay in the Word of God, and you can't do it by thinking, acting, and speaking like the world around you does. You will never overcome the reality of the world around you if you continue to act in a manner that would generate fear in your life.

If your faith is not working, the first place to look is in the words that you speak. Faith will not work without us speaking right words. Mark 11:23 tells us "Whosoever shall say unto this mountain, be thou removed, and be thou cast into the sea; and shall not doubt in his heart, but shall believe that those things which he saith shall come to pass; he shall have whatsoever he saith." Whatever you say consistently will come to pass. Your words are seeds, and what you plant is what you will harvest. You can bring to pass whatsoever you say and believe in your heart.

Doubt, from the Greek word *kiakrinomai*, means to hesitate, to waver, to doubt, or to differ. When a person's heart doesn't differ from what his mouth is saying, the combination of his heart and mouth in agreement will always make things happened.

Creative power is released when the heart and mouth get into agreement. This heart-mouth combination works on both the positive and negative sides of life. It can bring about the manifestation of healing in your body, salvation to your family, prosperity to your business, and growth to your local church. But the devil also knows how to use this principle against you.

The enemy knows that if he can fill your mind and heart with lies that you believe and then coax you into confessing those lies with your mouth, you will make those evil images come to pass in your life. That is exactly why the devil wants to fill your mind with lies and accusations. That is why he assaults your mind and emotions again and again. He knows that he only has to get you to embrace those lies and to start believing them.

Once you do that, you will soon start speaking those lies out of your mouth. And when you start speaking them with your mouth, it will only be a matter of time until they become your reality. Jesus said, "out of the abundance of the heart the mouth speaketh" (Matthew 12:34). So according to Jesus, whatever is in your heart is eventually going to come out of your mouth.

Great power is released when your heart and mouth start working together, so it's extremely important that you put the right things into your heart. Mark 11:23 promises that whatever you believe in your heart and say with your mouth will come to pass. But it doesn't just apply to Bible verses; it applies to anything you believe in your heart and say with your mouth. So if the devil can get you to believe and say wrong things, your own heart and mouth will cause those wrong confessions to come to pass.

You have got to actually get into the Word of God and do and say what the Bible says. Many times people hear the Word and agree with it, but they do not press in enough with their faith. They do not implement their faith and stay engaged until they receive what God has promised them.

This is why it is important for us to spend quality time in the Word of God. As you spend time meditating in the Word, your mind becomes renewed to God's way of thinking (Ephesians 4:23; Colossians 3:10). God's Word brings a supernatural cleansing that washes your mind and emotions from the contamination of the world, the memories of past experiences, and the lies that the enemy has tried to sow into your brain.

You will never receive your God-given blessings by walking around speaking like the world does, words of fear, lack, doubt, and unbelief, because those kind of words lead to thoughts that generate fear. Fear tolerated is faith contaminated, and contaminated faith simply does not work. So if you want to live in consistent victory, you must rid yourselves of that kind of thinking and think like God does.

> For my thoughts are not your thoughts, neither are your ways my ways, saith the Lord. For as the heavens are higher than the earth, so are my ways higher than your ways, and my thoughts higher than your thoughts. So shall my word be that goeth forth out of my mouth: it shall not return unto me void, but it shall accomplish that which I please, and it shall prosper in the thing whereto I sent it. (Isaiah 55:8–9, 11)

God has given us His Word to reveal His thoughts and His ways to us. He is telling us in His Word that it is His will that we prosper and be in health, that He takes great pleasure in our prosperity, that we are healed by Jesus' stripes, and that He desires for us to always prosper and be in good health (III John 2; Psalms 35:27; I Peter 2:24).

God's words and thoughts are simply amazing! They have the power to do what they say, but it is up to us to activate them by using the key that Jesus gave us in Matthew 6:31 where He instructs us to "take" thoughts by saying them. To keep your faith basket full, you must first make the decision to put and keep God's Word first place in your life. Second, think about what you are going to say, and third, always say what the Word of God says.

You must put the process to work in your life and stay with it until believing and speaking God's Word becomes automatic. You must get your heart so full of the Word that it becomes so much a part of you that when something confronts you, the Word will flow out of your mouth without any conscious effort.

6

THE NATURE OF FAITH

In II Thessalonians 1:3, Paul says that "your faith groweth exceedingly." So your faith can grow or shrink, which means that it can be greater or less than it is now. The following verses make this point.

> Luke 7:9: "great faith."
> Luke 12:28: "O ye of little faith."
> Romans 4:19: "being not weak in faith."
> Romans 4:20: "but was strong in faith."
> James 2:5: "rich in faith,"
> Acts 6:5: "Stephen, a man full of faith and of the Holy Ghost."

If faith can be weak or strong, little or great, then it can be less or it can be more. Faith is measurable.

James 2:22 (NAS) says that "You see that faith was working with his works, and as a result of the works, faith was perfected." I Timothy 1:5 talks about "unfeigned [sincere] faith," I Timothy 1:19 talks about "holding [fast to] faith," and I John 5:4 speaks of "overcoming faith."

Because the Bible says "in the mouth of two or three witnesses may every word be established," all of these verses will prove to you that faith is measurable (Matthew 18:16; II Corinthians 13:1).

This measure of faith that every believer has can be increased by feeding it with the Word of God or by exercising it and putting it into practice, or it can be left to decrease by ignoring the Word and not using it. Faith comes to you by hearing the Word of God. It will do you no good to ask God in prayer for more faith. He does not have it to give it to you. You simply need to hear the

Word of God and exercise your faith to get more faith. "So then faith cometh by hearing, and hearing by the word of God" (Romans 10:17).

God demands faith of us. He said in Hebrews 11:6 that "without faith it is impossible to please him; for he that cometh to God must believe that he is, and that he is a rewarder of them that diligently seek him."

God has placed the responsibility of getting and increasing your faith, above that measure of faith, squarely on your shoulders. God's Word is faith food, and the more of it that you digest into your spirit the more faith you are going to have to work with.

You have a measure of faith, and now is the time for you to start feeding yourself on the Word of God and exercising your faith daily. Set yourself a goal and spend a few minutes several times a day working on an ever increasing or growing faith. Take several scriptures that pertain to what you are believing God for and speak them out loud enough for you to hear yourself speak them several times a day. Start with something simple and work your way up to what you now think is impossible. According to Mark 11:23, "… and [he who] shall not doubt in his heart, but shall believe that those things which he saith shall come to pass; he shall have what he saith" (Mark 11:23).

In Romans 10:6–8, Paul says that the righteousness that is of faith says "the word is nigh thee, even in thy mouth and in thy heart." Notice that the Word of God is first in your mouth and then in your heart. God's Word becomes grafted into your heart as you speak it. There is nothing more important to your faith than declaring what God has said about you with your own voice. Giving voice to God's Word is a method of calling for things that God has given to you by promise but are not yet manifest into your life.

Don't judge yourself by other people. You don't know how long they have been believing God and exercising their faith. Start out where you are and work yourself up to where you want to be. You don't start climbing the stairs at the top step, and faith works the same way. As such, you can't believe above your measure of faith. Everybody starts on a level playing field with the same measure of faith, but some people feed and exercise their faith more and are able to do more with what they have.

Isaiah 1:19 tells us, "If ye be willing and obedient, ye shall eat the good of the land." So, just how willing are you to do what is right and to spend the required time in the Word of God to see your faith increased so that you can eat the good of the land?

Failure most often comes when people try to stretch their faith beyond what they have or are willing to work toward, and they give up, convinced that faith just doesn't work. Anytime you make a decision to try walking by faith, you are setting yourself up for failure. To live by faith is a lifestyle, and when you say that you are going to *try* living by faith, you are putting a time limit on it, because you are not persuaded that it will work.

Exercise your faith from where you are and allow yourself to grow in faith a little every day, and before you realize it, you will believe God for things that you never thought you could. Ephesians 3:10 says, "Now unto him that is able to do exceeding abundantly above all that we ask or think, according to the power that worketh in us."

That power that works in you is your faith. God will be able to do things in your life that will be exceeding abundantly above all that you can ask or think. That should be your goal—to see God working in your life way beyond anything that you can possibly conceive at this point in your life.

Faith doesn't cry for God to do something, it shouts and declares that it is already done! Faith is totally based on what God has already done for us.

7

HEART FAITH

Faith is of the heart and not the head. Notice, in Mark 11:23 it says, "… and shall not doubt in his heart, but shall believe." He shall believe in his heart. Romans 10:10 says, "For with the heart man believeth …" Faith is of the heart. The God-kind of faith is the faith of the heart, not of the head.

I Peter 3:4 says, "But let it be the hidden man of the heart …" The word heart, *kardia,* is the Greek word for the physical organ of the heart. Just as the physical organ of the heart is hidden from human sight, so the inner man is not visible to the natural eye.

The heart is the central vital organ of the body. Although the heart is invisible to natural sight, the human body cannot live without it. The heart has a direct impact on every part of the body as it pumps blood through its arteries and blood vessels.

The human spirit is similar to the natural heart. Both are invisible to the eye and are vital to life. James 2:26 tells us that where there is no spirit, the physical body dies, thus the spirit is the life-giving force within a human being.

The natural heart pumps blood into every part of the body and thereby influences a person's ability to live and function. Similarly, whatever is produced in the human spirit determines the ultimate outcome of a person's life. If a person's spirit is filled with darkness, it will pump darkness into every part of that person's life. On the other hand, if a person's spirit is filed with the life of God, it will pump life into every part of that person's being. Whatever is in the spirit is exactly what will be reproduced in a person's life and will be visible by his conduct.

That is why people act the way they do and that is why what you see and what you hear does make a difference in your life.

II Corinthians 4:16 (AMP) tells us, "Though our outer man is [progressively] decaying and wasting away, yet our inner self is being [progressively] renewed day after day." Here we can see that there is an outward man that is decaying and an inward man that is being renewed by the Word of God day by day. Just as the outward man requires us to spend time making our appearance more pleasing to look at we must also spend quality time fellowshipping with God getting ourselves into a position where we are more like God every day.

You are a spirit-being, you have a soul, and you live in a body. You contact the physical world with your physical body, you contact the spiritual world with your spirit, and you contact the intellectual world with your soul.

Faith is of the heart—the spirit or the inward man—and not of the head or of the body. Faith will work in your heart with doubt in your head. Don't let doubts in your mind defeat you! The Word says that "he shall not doubt in his heart" (Mark 11:23). It doesn't say anything about doubting in your head. It is heart faith that gets the job done and not head faith.

Proverbs 3:5 says to "Trust in the Lord with all thine heart; and lean not unto thine own understanding." Leaning on your own understanding is using your head to figure things out, and you are told here not to use your head but instead to trust God with your heart. I believe that this is one of the keys to walking with God in faith, because everybody has a tendency to try and figure things out on their own. To believe with the heart is to believe independently of human reasoning or sense knowledge. We must be very careful not to practice this in reverse, as it is human nature to trust in our own understanding and lean not to our heart.

James 1:5 tells us: "If any of you lack wisdom, let him ask of God." The word *wisdom* is from the Greek *sophias* and could describe enlightenment or insight, whereas the word *ask* is from the Greek *aiteo*, which means to be adamant in requesting and demanding assistance to meet tangible needs, such as food, shelter, and money. As one insists or demands that a certain need be met, he approaches his superior with great respect and honor. This word *aiteo* also expresses the idea that the one asking has a full expectation to receive what has been firmly requested.

Understand, when James tells us in this verse to *ask* God for the wisdom that we need, he understood that the Greek tense of the word *ask* has the meaning "to command." This clearly means God isn't suggesting that we come to Him for wisdom; He is commanding us to do so.

As such, God's wisdom is available to you all of the time just for the asking. Remember, God is no respecter of persons (Acts 10:34), and the same wisdom that God gave to Solomon is available to you and me.

I believe that I Kings 3:3–15 will give you a deeper understanding a deeper understanding of this.

Take the time and do a search for the word *wisdom*, especially in the books of Proverbs and Ecclesiastes, for a greater understanding of what God's wisdom is all about and what a great benefit having it is to us. Then when you are in need of God's wisdom, you simply need to ask Him for it. Just say:

Father, in Jesus' Name I ask for Your wisdom concerning [name the problem or situation]. I believe I receive Your wisdom, that same wisdom that You gave to Solomon, because Your Word says that You are no respecter of persons, and what things I desire of You when I pray, I simply have to believe that I receive them, and I shall have them. I believe I receive your wisdom and I receive it by faith now. (I Kings 4; Acts 10:34; Mark 11:24)

Now take a few minutes praying in the Spirit and listening to what He is direction you to do. Remember, God will not rebuke you or reprove you for asking for wisdom. You are His child, and He wants you to have all the wisdom that you need for life, health, and well-being. You will find God to be open-hearted and ready to answer any questions that you put to Him. But before He gives you those answers, He first wants you to come alongside Him, where He can share His love for you and fellowship with you (Hebrews 4:16).

As such, our faith should be in what God says and not in our feelings. Our feelings will almost always lead us to defeat when operating in the faith realm. Faith will work in your heart with doubt in your head. There is a contrast between head faith and heart faith.

Thomas' faith was a head faith; he wouldn't believe until he saw the nail print in Jesus' hand and put his finger in the print of the nail (John 20:24–29). Notice that Jesus called him faithless (verse 27), and He didn't commend or recommend Thomas' kind of faith, because anybody can have that kind of faith whether they are a saint or a sinner. He told Thomas to "be not faithless, but believing" (verse 29). Head faith is what your physical senses are telling your mind. Jesus said, "blessed [empowered to prosper] are they that have not seen, and yet have believed." God expects you to believe that you have things that you are not able to see with your physical senses.

In Romans 4, God gives us an account of Abraham and his faith. He chose to believe that what was spoken. There is probably no other subject as important to your walk in faith as the principle of calling things that are not as though they were (Romans 4:17). We see in Romans 4:17–22 that Abraham became fully persuaded that God would do what He had promised.

And the way he became fully persuaded was by calling those things which were not manifest as though they were.

In verse 17, we see: "(As it is written, I have made thee a father of many nations,) before him whom he believed, even God, who quickeneth the dead, and calleth those things which be not as though they were."

Here Paul is referring to Genesis 17. You will notice that God called Abram the father of nations before he had the promised child [Isaac], and He taught Abram to do the same. God changed Abram's name to Abraham, which means "father of nations, or multitude." This was the means He used to convince Abraham to call for what he did not yet have in reality. God had established it by promise, but Abram had to call it into reality by mixing faith with God's Word.

Every time that he said, "I am Abraham," he was calling things that were not yet manifest. Notice that he never denied that he was getting old. He didn't go around saying, "I'm not old," because he was old. But he said, "I am Abraham" (father of nations). This was God's method of helping him change his image, and it caused him to be fully persuaded.

Paul also gives us insight into this principle in I Corinthians 1:27–28.

> But God hath chosen the foolish things of the world to confound the wise; and God hath chosen the weak things of the world to confound the things which are mighty;
> And base things of the world, and things which are despised, hath God chosen, yea, and things which are not, to bring to naught things that are:

In other words, God uses spiritual forces that are not seen in order to nullify natural things that are seen. This is the Bible principle of calling things that are not as though they were.

Paul, inspired by the Spirit of God, is writing in Romans 4:17–21: "(As it is written, I have made you the father of many nations,) before him whom he believed, even God, who quickeneth the dead, and calleth those things which be not as though they were."

Notice, it says, "I have made you the father," not, I am going to do it, and he called those things which be not as though they were. It was a done deal! Abraham didn't have to do anything but believe God because it was his faith that caused him to confess those things "that be not as though they were." We put our faith into action by calling things "that be not as though they were" based on the promises of God.

You must be: "fully persuaded that what God has promised he is able to perform" (Romans 4:21). You must always base your confession of faith on one of God's promises. You never base your confession a want or a desire.

We see an example here in the life of Abraham:

> Who against hope believed in hope, that he might become the father of many nations, according to that which was spoken, so shall thy seed be. And being not weak in faith, he considered not his own body now dead, when he was about an hundred years old, neither yet the deadness of Sarah's womb;
>
> He staggered not at the promise of God through unbelief; but was strong in faith, giving glory to God;
>
> And being fully persuaded that, what he had promised, he was able also to perform. (Romans 4:18 – 20)

The promise to Abram is found in Genesis 17:5–7:

> Neither shall thy name any more be called Abram, but thy name shall be Abraham: for a father of many nations have I made thee.
>
> And I will make thee exceeding fruitful, and I will make nations of thee, and kings shall come out of thee.
>
> And I will establish my covenant between me and thee and thy seed after thee in their generations for an everlasting covenant, to be a God unto thee, and to thy seed after thee.

Faith is always in the present tense and is never in the future tense. Future-tense faith is nothing but hoping for something. Hebrews 11:1 says: "Now faith is the substance of things hoped for, the evidence of things not seen." If it is not now, it is not faith! Faith is now, present tense. Being strong in faith is giving glory to God, and when you are fully persuaded that God is able to do what he has promised, your faith will be credited to you for righteousness (Isaiah 58:8; Romans 4:21–22).

In Romans 4:19 –22 (AMP) we see where Abraham:

> … did not weaken in faith when he considered the [utter] impotence of his own body, which was as good as dead because he was about a hundred years old, or [when he considered] the barrenness of Sarah's [deadened] womb.

No unbelief or distrust made him waver (doubtingly question) concerning the promise of God, but he grew strong and was empowered by faith as he gave praise and glory to God.

Fully satisfied and assured that God was able and mighty to keep His word and to do what He had promised.

That is why his faith was credited to him as righteousness (right standing with God).

As such, your righteousness will be imputed to you as you believe God and give praise and glory to Him. "For he hath made him to be sin for us, who knew no sin; that we might be made the righteousness of God in him" (II Corinthians 5:17).

We are made the righteousness of God in Christ Jesus, and this righteousness brings peace, fellowship, and faith and restores sonship, which will allow you to walk and talk with God in fellowship like Adam experienced before the fall.

Your righteousness is your bill of rights in the Kingdom of God. And you are "to awake to righteousness, and sin not," because righteousness does not come by the way you act. It is in the nature of God, and when you join in with that nature, your actions will become right, because that right way of acting is your conduct, which is holiness (I Corinthians 15:34).

Understanding your righteousness is the key to participating in all that Jesus obtained for you at the cross. And to understand your righteousness you are required to simply receive what Jesus has done for you by faith. Jesus took that old sin nature away and made you a new creature in Christ. One that can come boldly to the throne of grace and fellowship with the Father just like Adam did in the garden (II Corinthians 5:17; Hebrews 4:16).

How does God see you? He sees you through the blood of Jesus Christ. Therefore, there is no condemnation to those who are in Christ Jesus, which makes you qualified to sit together in heavenly places in Christ Jesus (Ephesians 2:6).

When you awake to your righteousness, it will awaken a new boldness on the inside, and you will see yourself as God sees you. This will allow you to walk and talk to God on a father-son basis. Remember, God's ears are open to the righteous and "the effectual fervent prayer of a righteousness man availeth much" (James 5:16).

A righteous man is not absolutely perfect, but he is a person who is doing good things, and his prayers are being answered. If he misses it, he has only to sincerely say, "Jesus, I'm sorry." And the blood of Jesus comes in like a flood to wipe the slate clean!

That is why Isaiah 32:17 tells us that "the work of the righteous shall be peace; and the effect of righteousness quietness and assurance forever."

Righteousness is not conduct; it is your right-standing with God, and it allows you to live with God in peace and harmony forever. It is what gives you the ability to stand in the presence of a holy God without a sense of guilt, fear, inferiority, or condemnation. And it enables you to "come boldly unto the throne of grace, that you may obtain mercy, and find grace to help in time of need" (Hebrews 4:16).

Good conduct does not produce righteousness. Righteousness produces good conduct, because it carries with it all the authority and power you'll ever need to overcome sin.

To receive what you have a right to receive according to the Word of God, you must believe that you are the righteousness of God. Experiencing prosperity, healing, and victory will always be a problem if righteousness never becomes a reality in your life. You have got to understand your rights according to the Word of God and then exercise these rights given to you in the New Testament. As the righteousness of God, you have a blood-bought right to pray and get answers to your prayers, and it is vital for you to understand righteousness and receive it in order to prosper in God in this life.

Your righteousness is a gift. You can't work for it, earn it, or do good deeds to obtain it. You have to be accounted and declared righteous by God. The day you received Jesus into your life as Lord and personal Savior, God declared you righteous. By faith, you received your salvation, and all of these rights were given to you as the righteousness of God. The right to be healed, delivered, prospered, favored, and saved is all yours through faith in the blood of Jesus and by your faith in the righteousness of God.

What does righteousness mean? In its simplest form, it means "right standing with God." When you are righteous, you are right with God. You stand in equality with Him. You have an authority and a right to stand before God and talk to Him just like you would talk to your own earthly father. To be righteous, then, means that God has declared you in equality with Himself, and you can go to Him and expect to receive from Him, because you are right with Him. Righteousness is the ability to stand in the Father's presence without the sense of guilt, fear, inferiority, or condemnation.

Romans 5:17 explains a little better just what Jesus accomplished for us at the cross: "For if by one man's offence death reined by one; much more they which receive abundance of grace and of the gift of righteousness shall reign in life by one, Jesus Christ."

Jesus' blood purchased the forgiveness for all of mankind's sins. Because of Adam's disobedience, sin entered the world, and death was passed on to all men. But just as sin entered the world through Adam, the gift of God came into the world through the obedience of Jesus Christ. Now the grace of God and the free gift of righteousness abound to all who have called upon Jesus Christ to be their Lord and Savior. As such, every believer has the glorious privilege of reigning in life as a joint heir with Jesus Himself.

If you have made Jesus the Lord of your life, you are no longer just an old sinner, but a new creation created in Christ Jesus. You have received an abundance of grace and the gift of righteousness. Instead of being a slave to sin, you have been born again into a royal family and have been given the right to reign in life as a king! (II Corinthians 5:17–21).

You have been put in a position of authority over your life and circumstances. You are spiritual royalty.

Spiritual royalty works in much the same way that earthly royalty does. The heir of a king has the same legal rights and privileges as the king himself. Even though the heir may be just a child and is still being tutored, he is nevertheless king of the land. He has the necessary right and authority to rule.

As such, Romans 8:16–17 and Galatians 4:7 explain that:

> The Spirit itself beareth witness with our spirit, that we are the children of God:
> And if children, then heirs; heirs of God, and joint-heirs with Christ; if so be that we suffer with him, that we may be also glorified together.
>
> Wherefore thou art no more a servant, but a son; and if a son, then an heir of God through Christ.

And Colossians 1:12–13 explains why we are to be:

> Giving thanks unto the Father, which hath made us meet [fit] to be partakers of the inheritance of the saints in light:
> Who hath delivered us from the power of darkness, and hath translated us into the kingdom of his dear Son:

God has made us "fit to be partakers of the inheritance of the saints in light" and has "translated us into of the kingdom of his dear Son." He has already done it. He has translated us out of the kingdom and authority of darkness and into His kingdom of light. He has delivered us out of the control of our adversary, and the devil has no authority over us whatsoever. Jesus defeated him at Calvary and took from him his ability to hold us captive (Colossians 2:15; Matthew 28:18).

II Corinthians 5:17 tells us: "Therefore if any man be in Christ, he is a new creature: old things are passed away; behold all things are become new."

And if you have become that new creature in Christ, certain things are expected of you.

> That ye put off concerning the former conversation the old man, which is corrupt according to the deceitful lusts;
>
> And be renewed in the spirit of your mind;
>
> And that ye put on the new man, which after God is created in righteousness and true holiness. (Ephesians 4:22–24)

> For in Him [in Christ] the whole fullness of Diety (the Godhead) continues to dwell in bodily form [giving complete expression of the divine nature].
>
> And you are in Him, made full and having come to fullness of life [in Christ you too are filled with the Godhead—Father, Son and Holy Spirit—and reach full spiritual stature]. And He is the Head of all rule and authority [of every angelic principality and power].
>
> In Him also you were circumcised with a circumcision not made with hands, but in a [spiritual] circumcision [performed by] Christ by stripping off the body of the flesh (the whole corrupt, carnal nature with its passions and lusts).
>
> [Thus you were circumcised when] you were buried with Him in [your] baptism, in which you were also raised with Him [to a new life] through [your] faith in the workings of God [as displayed] when He raised Him up from the dead.
>
> And you who were dead in trespasses and in the uncircumcision of your flesh (your sensuality, your sinful carnal nature), [God] brought to life together with [Christ], having [freely] forgiven us all our transgressions.
>
> Having cancelled and blotted out and wiped away the handwriting of the note (bond) with its legal decrees and demands which were in force and stood against us (hostile to us). This [note with its regulations, decrees, and demands] He set aside and cleared completely out of our way by nailing it to [His] cross.
>
> [God] disarmed the principalities and powers that were ranged against us and made a bold display and public

example of them in triumphing over them in Him and in it [the cross].
(Colossians 2:9–15 AMP)

It's important to note that the Amplified Bible uses the word *disarmed* in verse 15, which means several things: (1) He took away his weapons, (2) He deprived him of his ability to harm, (3) He overcame his hostility against us, and (4) He reduced his power and ability to zero.

Jesus destroyed Satan's power over us at Calvary. Hebrews 2:14 explains "that through death he might destroy him that had the power of death, that is, the devil" (AMP). The Rotherham Translation states, "bring to naught and make of no effect. He paralyzed his death dealing power.

Satan is helpless against you when you know that you have been delivered from his control. I John 2:14 states, "ye are strong, and the word of God abideth in you, and ye have overcome the wicked one."

No matter what comes against you, it will not succeed if you stand in the authority that Jesus has conferred upon you. Luke 10:19 states, "Behold, I give unto you power to tread on serpents and scorpions and over all the power of the enemy, and nothing shall by any means hurt you."

Jesus has shattered Satan's power over you, and you should never fear him again. It's time for you to begin acting as if you truly believe this. When you do, then "you cannot be defeated." Trials and adversities may come your way, but they should not keep you from living a victorious life. Psalms 34:19 (AMP) states, "Many evils confront the [consistently] righteous, but the Lord delivers him out of them all."

God never intended for you to fail, and nothing makes Him happier than to see you overcoming everything that Satan throws your way. If you are facing adversity, just refuse to give up. For with God on your side, you cannot be defeated!

You may feel as if you can't take anymore, but if you'll refuse to give up, then God will make a way. 2 Corinthians 1:10 (AMP) states, "For it is he Who rescued and saved us.... He will again deliver us [from danger and destruction and draw us to Himself]."

God turns Satan's setbacks into your victories. 2 Corinthians 4:9 (AMP) states, "we are struck down ... but never struck out and destroyed."

The Word tells us that we are "beyond defeat." When we know this and act upon it, Satan cannot keep us from overcoming all of his attacks against us. Satan is not all-powerful as he would have you believe.

We are the ones with the power, but it does us little good if we refuse to use it. Luke 24:49 states that we are "endued with power from on high." *Endued* means: "to put on and to be clothed with." This means that we have to wear our power and authority like we would a coat. It also means "to be skilled." This indicates that we should practice using our power and authority and not let it lay dormant.

Ephesians 6:10–18 tells us to:

> Finally, my brethren, be strong in the Lord and in the power of his might.
>
> For we wrestle not against flesh and blood, but against principalities, against powers, against the rulers of the darkness of the world, against spiritual wickedness in high places.
>
> Wherefore take unto you the whole armour of God, that ye may be able to withstand in the evil day, and having done all, to stand.
>
> Stand therefore, having your loins girt about with truth, and having on the breastplate of righteousness;
>
> And your feet shod with the preparation of the gospel of peace;
>
> Above all, taking the shield of faith, wherewith ye shall be able to quench all the fiery darts of the wicked.
>
> And take the helmet of salvation, and the sword of the Spirit, which is the word of God:
>
> Praying always with all prayer and supplication in the Spirit, and watching thereunto with all perseverance and supplication for all saints.

Ephesians 6:10-18 is explained further in chapter 13, The fullness of the Blessing.

Hebrews 4:12 tells us, "For the Word of God is quick, and powerful, and sharper than any twoedged sword, piercing even to the dividing asunder of soul and spirit, and of the joints and marrow, and is a discerner of the thoughts and intents of the heart." And when the sword of the spirit comes flying out of your mouth, it cuts the devil right to the bone, which makes him mighty unhappy. But God is on your side, and the devil can't stop you unless you let him (Isaiah 54:17). Your faith is a spiritual force that the devil can't compete with, but he will try to get you to give it up, and his method is always based on natural situations called distractions. He will try to use situations, circumstances, and people to steer you away from your confession, your childlike faith, and doing what you known is right. But it is vitally important for you to remember that you have your God-given power and authority to stay the course, no matter what.

If Satan is prevailing over you and defeating you, then it has to be for one of the following reasons: lack of knowledge of your authority over him, knowing your authority but failing to act upon it, or knowing and using your authority but giving up too quickly because you've become deceived into thinking that you cannot win.

Defeat is not in God's plan for your life. Deuteronomy 28:13 says, "And the lord will make thee the head, and not the tail; and thou shall be above only, and thou shalt not be beneath."

The same Jesus that was anointed by God to do serious damage to the devil on the cross of Calvary is the very same Jesus who now lives in you. That means you have the power in you! Remind yourself of it every day. It's your choice. It is part of your righteousness to know your rights as a son of God and claim them!

Ephesians 2:10 tells us: "For we are his workmanship, created in Christ Jesus unto good works, which God hath before ordained that we should walk in them." We find that by being translated, we have actually been re-created (restored) to where we once were (II Corinthians 5:17).

"God hath before ordained." In other words, God predestined, preordained, and pre-created. He brought us back to the place where we came into being before the foundation of the world. He brought us back to where He chose us, and He sees us where we belong, back where He had us at the very beginning before Adam sinned (Ephesians 1:4).

God is your Father, and you are His child. You have His dominion, His Name, His Spirit, and His righteousness. Everything that is His is yours.

Colossians 1:21–22 explains: "… yet now hath he reconciled. In the body of his flesh through death, to present you holy and unblameable and unreproveable in his sight." This allows us to come boldly to the throne of grace and say, "I am reconciled. I belong here. This is my place. I am the righteousness of God! My Father loves me, and I love Him" (Hebrews 4:16).

2 Peter 1:4 tells us: "Whereby are given unto us exceeding great and precious promises: that by these ye might be partakers of the divine nature, having escaped the corruption that is in the world through lust." (Pressure).

The fact that you've been made the righteousness of God in Christ Jesus needs to be as real to you as the air you breathe, and the fact that you are a partaker of the divine nature of God through His great and precious promises needs to be as real to you as the sun coming up every morning.

God has given you the right to walk into His presence without a sense of shame, guilt, sin, or a lack of belonging there. That's because you are righteous. And you were made righteous the moment you were born again.

Always remember:

> God hath chosen the foolish things of the world to confound
> the wise; and God hath chosen the weak things of the world
> to confound the things which are mighty;
>> And base things of the world, and things which are
> despised, hath God chosen, yea, and things which are not,
> to bring to nought things that are:
>> That no flesh should glory in his presence.
>> But of him are ye in Christ Jesus, who of God is made
> unto us wisdom, and righteousness, and sanctification, and
> redemption.
>> That according as it is written, He that glorieth, let him
> glory in the Lord. (I Corinthians 1:27–31)

> Christ hath redeemed us from the curse of the law, being
> made a curse for us: for it is written, Cursed is every one that
> hangeth on a tree:
>> That the blessings of Abraham might come on the
> Gentiles through Jesus Christ; that we might receive the
> promise of the Spirit through faith. (Galatians 3:13–14)

Redeemed means to release on receipt of ransom. It denotes a buyout, similar to that of a slave owner who purchases a slave for the sole purpose of setting him free. To be redeemed then means to be delivered. Delivered from sin, sickness, poverty and spiritual death.

Christ has already redeemed us from the curse and delivered us from poverty, sin, sickness, and spiritual death. We are not going to be redeemed. We are already redeemed—right now. Jesus paid the price for all of us.

Jesus gave Himself for us to redeem us from all iniquity. He did not redeem us with corruptible things like silver and gold but with His precious blood, as that of a lamb without spot or blemish (I Peter 1:18–19).

The following scriptures are filled with references to the things that Jesus has done for you. Here is a list of just some of them:

1 Timothy 2:5–6: "For there is one God, and one mediator between God and men, the man Christ Jesus; Who gave himself a ransom for all, to be testified in due time."

Titus 2:13–14: "… Jesus Christ; Who gave himself for us, that he might redeem us from all iniquity, and purify unto himself a peculiar people …"

Colossians 1:12–14 (AMP): "Who has qualified and made us fit to share the portion which is the inheritance of the saints (God's holy people) in the

Light. [The Father] has delivered and drawn us to Himself out of the control and dominion of darkness and has transferred us into the kingdom of the Son of His love. In whom we have our redemption through His blood [which means] the forgiveness of our sins."

2 Corinthians 2:14 (AMP): "But thanks be to God, Who in Christ always leads us in triumph [as trophies of Christ's victory] and through us spreads and makes evident the fragrance of the knowledge of God everywhere."

Revelation 1:6: "And hath made us kings and priests unto God and his Father ..."

Revelation 1:6 (AMP): "And formed us into a kingdom (a royal race), priests to His God and Father ..."

1 John 3:8: "He that committeth sin is of the devil; for the devil sinneth from the beginning. For this purpose the Son of God was manifested, that he might destroy the works of the devil."

The Greek word for destroy is *luo*, which means to loosen, undo, or dissolve. Jesus has loosened the shackles of sin, and all we have to do is walk in our freedom.

In Psalms 107:2 we are directed to "Let the redeemed of the Lord say so, whom he hath redeemed from the hand of the enemy."

So say, "I am redeemed! I am redeemed from poverty, sickness, sin, and spiritual death. Praise God, I have been redeemed from the hand of the enemy by the blood of Jesus!"

It's important to remember that if you have been living in defeat, you may find the fact that you've been made a king just a little hard to believe. It may look to you like poverty, sickness, or sin is ruling your life. But if that's the case, you must realize that you've actually been living in deceit not defeat. By blinding you to the royal righteousness that God has placed within you, Satan has tricked you into surrendering your true authority.

If you have been living in bondage to sin and circumstances, the problem is not that God needs to do something more to set you free. He's done all that it takes to set you free by giving you all the rights and privileges that Jesus had when He was on the earth, including the power of the Holy Spirit (Acts 10:38).

Now He is waiting on you to stand in faith and assert those rights and privileges. He's waiting on you to take His Word and authority and show Satan just who's boss. Until you dig in your heels and demand your spiritual rights in Jesus' Name, Satan is going to walk all over you.

You have a right to walk in victory, because Jesus gave you that right. It makes no difference whether you feel righteous or not; you are righteous because God has made you righteous. Your victory will come through a revelation of this, and when you get it, then and only then will you start getting results in your personal life, your business affairs, and in all areas of your life.

I Corinthians 15:34 directs us to "Awake to righteousness and sin not." To awake to righteousness means to become aware that you have been made the righteousness of God in Jesus Christ.

If you have turned your back on a sinful life and have given yourself to Jesus Christ, then you have been placed in right-standing with Almighty God through the sacrifice of Jesus at Calvary—the cross. When you awake to your righteousness, you will have to let go of whatever sin may be trying to hang onto you, you will have to let it go.

A good scripture to read and meditate on for this is 2 Corinthians 4. Verse 4 tells us: "In whom the god of this world (Satan) hath blinded the minds of them which believe not, least the light of the glorious gospel of Christ, who is the image of God, should shine unto them."

As long as Satan can convince you that you don't have any right to the things of God, he can keep you under his thumb, and sin will control your life. But when you awake to righteousness, you will realize that Satan is a defeated foe. It is then that the struggle will be over because "greater is he that is in you, than he that is in the world" (I John 4:4).

You can dominate sin and Satan no matter what the circumstances.

If there is a situation that is dominating you rather than you dominating it, go to the Word of God. Spend time in prayer and meditation in the word. The Lord will lead you through the Word and through His still small voice just as He promised in John 10:27 when He said: "My sheep hear my voice."

You'll then know how to take control over the problem by the leadership of the Holy Spirit. Jesus said that when the Spirit of Truth came, He would take the things of God and reveal them to us (John 14:26).

You can reign in every area of life if you will diligently do the following:

1. Find the will of God in your situation by prayer and meditation in the word of God.
2. Once you have found the will of God, confer no longer with flesh and blood.
3. Get your job done at all costs. Don't allow anything or anyone to stand in the way of God's will.

Before you can take these three steps, however, you must first reclaim your royal heritage, never again to surrender it to the enemy. You must be ready to stand stubbornly on the rights and privileges you've been given as a child of the King. Not for just an hour or a day, but for a lifetime.

Remember, as a born-again son of God, "You are more than a conqueror through Him who loved us" (Romans 8:37). And we always triumph over opposition (II Corinthians 2:14).

You couldn't be a conqueror if there wasn't something to conquer. A conqueror is one who consistently wins in battle, one who defeats his enemy and renders him to be powerless to renew the attack. He is one who is permanently registered on the winning side. Conquerors are made such by God. They are people who consistently win battles with God's backing. They do not know defeat, because the hand of the Lord is on them. This is the Spirit of the Lord in action. This is the anointing for conquest. As long as the hand of the Lord is on you, your victory is established.

Christ in you makes you more than a conqueror, and to be more than a conqueror means you will also transform trials into incredible faith opportunities. For it is always "God, which always causeth us to triumph in Christ" (II Corinthians 2:14). Remember, in Him there is only one end to every challenge: triumph and conquest.

Conquerors have two major weapons: fearlessness (courage) and the presence of God. In this world the fearless reign and the fearful live as slaves. The man who conquers is the one who refuses to give in to fear. (Fear is the direct opposite of faith.) If you do not fear, you will always conquer your enemies. Fearlessness provides us with the backbone for exploits and achievements.

Luke 1:37 AMP tells us, "For with God nothing is ever impossible and no word from God shall be without power or impossible of fulfillment." Remember this as you meditate the following verses!

1 Peter 3:12: "The eyes of the Lord are over the righteous, and his ears are open unto their prayers: but the face of the Lord is against them that do evil."

Psalms 34:15, 17, 19: "The eyes of the Lord are upon the righteous, and his ears are open to their cry.

The righteous cry, and the Lord heareth, and delivereth them out of all their troubles.

Many are the afflictions of the righteous: but the Lord delivereth him out of them all."

Proverbs 10–14: "… the desire of the righteous shall be granted."

Proverbs 10–25: "… the righteous is an everlasting foundation."

Proverbs 11:3: "… the righteous shall be recompensed in the earth."

Proverbs 2:10: "… righteousness delivereth from death."

Proverbs 11:8: "The righteous is delivered out of trouble."

1 Peter 3:12: "For the eyes of the Lord are over the righteous and His ears are open unto their prayers: but the face of the Lord is against them that do evil."

Isaiah 3:10 (AMP): "Say to the righteous that it shall be well with them, for they shall eat the fruit of their deeds. Woe to the wicked! It shall be ill with him, for what his hands have done shall be done to him."

Proverbs 29:2: "When the righteous are in authority, the people rejoice: but when the wicked beareth rule, the people morn."

Proverbs 27:7: "The righteous considereth the cause of the poor: but the wicked reguardeth not to know it."

Proverbs 28:27: "He that giveth unto the poor shall not lack: but he that hideth his eyes shall have many a curse."

2 Thessalonians 1:6–9: "Seeing it is a righteous thing with God to recompense tribulation to them that trouble you.

And to you who are troubled rest with us, when the Lord Jesus shall be revealed from heaven with his mighty angles.

In flaming fire taking vengeance on them that know not God, and that obey not the gospel of our Lord Jesus Christ.

Who shall be punished with everlasting destruction from the presence of the Lord, and from the glory of his power?"

Romans 1:16–17: "For I am not ashamed of the gospel of Christ: for it is the power of God unto salvation to every one that believeth; to the Jew first, and also to the Greek.

For therein (in the Word) is the righteousness of God revealed from faith to faith: as it is written, the just shall live by faith."

Romans 10:4–10: "For Christ is the end of the law for righteousness to every one that believeth.

For Moses describeth the righteousness which is of the law, that the man which doeth those things shall live by them.

But the righteousness which is of faith speaketh on this wise, Say not in thine heart, Who shall ascend into heaven? (That is, to bring Christ down from above:)

Or, Who shall descend unto the deep? (that is, to bring up Christ again from the dead).

But what saith it? The word is nigh thee, even in thy mouth, and in thy heart: that is, the word of faith which we preach;

That if thou shalt confess with thy mouth the Lord Jesus, and shalt believe in thine heart that God hath raised him from the dead, thou shalt be saved.

For with the heart man believeth unto righteousness; and with the mouth confession is made unto salvation."

Proverbs 18:10: "The name of the Lord is a strong tower: the righteous runneth into it, and is safe."

Isaiah 43:26: "Put me in remembrance: let us plead together: declare thou, that thou mayest be justified."

"Put God in remembrance of the covenant by quoting his word back to him which will also cause your faith to be built up and allow you to walk in victory."

THE KEY TO UNDERSTANDING YOUR RIGHTEOUSNESS

> My Son, if thou wilt receive my words, and hide my commandments with thee;
>
> So that thou incline thine ear unto wisdom, and apply thine heart to understanding;
>
> Yea, if thou criest after knowledge, and lifteth up thy voice for understanding.
>
> If thou seekest her as silver, and searchest for her as for hid treasures;
>
> Then shalt thou understand the fear of the Lord, and find the knowledge of God.
>
> For the Lord giveth wisdom: out of his mouth cometh knowledge and understanding.
>
> He layeth up sound wisdom for the righteous: he is a buckler to them that walk uprightly.
>
> He keepeth the paths of judgment, and preserveth the way of his saints.
>
> Then shalt thou understand righteousness, and judgment, and equity (Proverbs 2:1–9)

God wants to reveal every good path to you. He has laid up sound wisdom that will enable you to live up to your full potential. Proverbs 3:5–6 reveals how you can find your pathway in life: "Trust in the Lord with all thine heart; and lean not unto thine own understanding. In all thy ways acknowledge Him, and He shall direct thy paths."

> Their Righteousness is of Me, saith the Lord!
>
> Father, thank You for Your promises. I praise You that You are the Lord, my Redeemer.

Your kindness and the covenant of Your peace shall never depart from me.

All my borders are laid with pleasant stones.

All my children are taught of You, and great is the peace of my children.

I am established in Your righteousness. Even though fear, oppression, and terror shall gather together, they are not from You. I'll not receive them! They shall fall for my sake!

Fall, fear! Fall, oppression! Fall, terror! You're not from God, and you'll not come near me! Jesus has defeated the devil and all of his works.

No weapon that is formed against thee shall prosper!

Every tongue that rises against me shall be condemned. This is my inheritance and my blood—bought right in Jesus. He is my righteousness. The Lord says so! (Isaiah 54:8–17).

TWO KINDS OF RIGHTEOUSNESS

Webster's Second New College Dictionary defines righteousness as "meeting the standards of what is right and just." But, God is the One who sets these standards, and when we meet them, we are said to be righteous, or acceptable, and in right relationship with Him. Basically, the Bible talks about two kinds of righteousness. The first kind is the one we try to gain by keeping the law or by doing "good works." It is a righteousness we attempt to earn by following a system of rules and regulations. But this type of righteousness is unacceptable to God and brings frustration, aggravation, and disappointment to the person trying to earn it. According to Galatians 3:10 (AMP), "all who depend on the law [who are seeking to be justified by obedience to the law of rituals] are under a curse and doomed to disappointment and destruction.

When we strive to be acceptable to God by what we do, we are relying on our flesh to make us righteous. And according to the Word, this is impossible to do because nothing good dwells in our flesh (Romans 7:18). Isaiah 64:6 says, "But we are all as an unclean thing and all our righteousness are as filthy rags; and we all do fade as a leaf; and our iniquities like the wind, have taken us away."

The Amplified Bible puts it this way: "For we have all become as one who is unclean [ceremonially, as a leper], and all our righteousness—our best deeds of rightness and justice—are as filthy rags or a polluted garment. We all fade as a leaf, and our iniquities, like the wind, take us away [far from God's favor, hurrying us to destruction]."

But, on the other hand, there is a righteousness that is acceptable to God, and it is found in Christ Jesus. It cannot be earned and has absolutely nothing to do with what we do. It is totally based on what Jesus did. This genuine righteousness can only be received as a gift from God through believing in the death, burial, and resurrection of Jesus Christ (Romans 10:9). "For He hath made Him to be sin for us, who knew no sin; that we might be made the righteousness of God in him" (II Corinthians 5:21).

The Amplified version states the same passage this way: "For our sake He made Christ [virtually] to be sin who knew no sin, so that in and through Him we might become [endued with, viewed as in and examples of] the righteousness of God—what we ought to be, approved and acceptable and in right relationship with Him, by His goodness."

If we could work our way into a right relationship with God by exhibiting right behavior, Jesus would never have had to come to die. But because we can't work our way into a right relationship with Him, He sent His Son, Jesus, to meet the full requirements of His justice. Jesus became the manifestation of our righteousness, thus making us in right standing with God.

1 Corinthians 1:30 says, "But of Him are you in Christ Jesus, who of God is made unto us wisdom, and righteousness, and sanctification, and redemption. And the Amplified version says, "But it is from Him that you have your life in Christ Jesus, Whom God made our Wisdom from God, [that is, revealed to us a knowledge of the divine plan of salvation previously hidden, manifesting itself as] our Righteousness [thus making us upright and putting us in right standing with God]; and our Consecration [making us pure and holy]; and our Redemption [providing our ransom from eternal penalty for sin]."

We see a good example of not relying on our flesh in Philippians 3:4–9:

> Though I might also have confidence in the flesh. If any other man thinketh that he hath whereof he might trust in the flesh, I more:
>
> Circumcised the eighth day, of the stock of Israel, of the tribe of Benjamin, an Hebrew of the Hebrews; as touching the law, a Pharisee;
>
> Concerning zeal, persecuting the church; touching the righteousness which is in the law, blameless.
>
> But what things were gain to me, those I counted loss for Christ.

> Yea doubtless, and I count all things but loss for the Excellency of the knowledge of Christ Jesus my Lord: for whom I have suffered the loss of all things, and do count them but dung, that I may win Christ.
>
> And be found in him, not having mine own righteousness, which is of the law, but that which is through the faith of Christ, the righteousness which is of God by faith.

If there was anyone who had a "right" to claim that he was righteous because of following the law, it was Paul. He was circumcised when he was eight days old, from the tribe of Benjamin, and a Hebrew of Hebrews. And as for observing the law, he was a Pharisee, which means that he kept the law to the letter, and there was no fault found in him. Even though he had all these things going for him in the natural, or in the flesh, he counted them all as a loss.

The only way that we can possess this genuine righteousness is by believing in Jesus Christ. This means that we must believe that Jesus came and died on the cross in our place, taking our punishment for all of our past, present, and future sins. And on the third day, He rose from the dead, having victory over the world, the flesh, and the devil. For it is through this faith that we are made the righteousness of God in Christ Jesus (I Corinthians 15:3–4).

In Philippians 3:3 (AMP), we are told: "For we [Christians] are the true circumcision, who worship God in spirit and by the Spirit, and exult and glory and pride ourselves in Jesus Christ, and put no confidence or dependence [on what we are] in the flesh and on outward privileges and physical advantages and external appearances."

> For we [not relying on the law], through the (Holy) Spirit's [help] by faith anticipate and wait for the blessing and good for which our righteousness and right standing with God—our conformity to His will in purpose, thought and action—[causes us] to hope.
>
> For [if we are] in Christ Jesus, neither circumcision nor uncircumcision counts for anything, but only faith activated and energized and expressed and working through love. (Galatians 5:5–6 AMP)

Understanding how we are made righteous takes time. Little by little and from faith to faith, we learn to use patience for this revelation to move from our heads to our hearts. Our lives are filled with many faults, and we have a tendency to try to do things good and win God's approval, but we can never measure up. It will just cause us to suffer condemnation and guilt.

We must remember that we are not going to do everything right all of the time. We must give ourselves permission to be human beings and stop trying to be something that we are not. We must get up every morning and do the best that we can. When we make a mistake, we must run to God, not away from Him. If we confess our mistakes to God, he will take care of it, because He loves us that much.

> If we [freely] admit that we have sinned and confess our sins, He is faithful and just [true to His own nature and promises] and will forgive our sins (dismiss our lawlessness) and continuously cleanse us from all unrighteousness— everything not in conformity to His will in purpose, thought and action. (I John 1:9 AMP)

We should have sorrow over the sins we commit, but we can't remain sorrowful and allow the enemy to bombard us with guilt and condemnation. God knows all of our weaknesses and every mistake we're ever going to make. He knew them before we were born, and He still approved of us.

Jeremiah 1:5 (AMP) tells us: "Before I formed you in the womb I knew and approved of you [as My chosen instrument], and before you were born I separated and set you apart, consecrating you, and I appointed you a prophet to the nations." And Psalms 139:16 AMP says, "Your eyes saw my unformed substance, and in Your book all the days of my life were written, before ever they took shape, when as yet there was none of them."

If God knew us before we were born, and He recorded all the days of our lives before they took place, He obviously knows every mess and mistake we're ever going to make. Yet, He still chose to "birth us" into His family.

God doesn't expect us to never make any mistakes. He is committed to taking care of us and helping us grow through every mistake we make.

We are not a surprise to God! Just remember, when you do make mistakes, run to God, not away from Him. He will always welcome you back with open arms. He loves you that much.

According to Isaiah 32:17, "And the work of righteousness shall be peace; and the effect of righteousness quietness and assurance for ever." In other words, doing right—or doing what is righteous—has power. It has the power to work peace, quietness, and assurance in your life.

The word "peace" in the above verse in Hebrew can be translated as "fullness, wholeness, completeness, prosperity" and has a literal definition of "nothing missing, nothing broken."

So the above verse is telling us: "The work of righteousness shall be [fullness, wholeness, completeness, and prosperity with nothing missing and nothing broken]; and the effect of righteousness quietness and assurance for ever."

That is a mouthful of God's covenant promises, but it's all for any person who will choose to do the right thing.

Righteousness simply means "rightness." It is the state of being right. It is also the act of doing what is right, which is where it so closely ties into the idea of honor.

Read Genesis chapters 37, 39, 40, and 41 for a good example of what I mean. Joseph had many opportunities but always chose to do what was right and honorable even in situations where fear could have taken over. And because he always did what was right, no matter how terrible the situation, he always came out prospering. Even in the most unlikely of circumstances, the force of righteousness was constantly going before him, straightening out problems, giving him peace, and causing him to prosper.

Notice also that Isaiah 32:17 says one of the effects of righteousness is assurance. Assurance, or confidence, can only come from knowing that we are righteous. It comes from knowing we have the God-given ability to stand in the presence of our heavenly Father totally and completely at peace and free from fear without a sense of guilt, condemnation, or inferiority. We can stand in the presence of a Holy God as though sin never existed in our lives. But righteousness is also our ability to stand in the face of Satan without fear and boldly resist him, expecting him to flee. Righteousness always turns the table on the devil, which is why he could never keep Joseph down.

This kind of boldness before God and this kind of boldness before the devil are the reality of our own developed goodness or holiness here. Our good deeds and failed attempts at trying to clean ourselves up are as "filthy rags" (Isaiah 64:6).

But God says, "Awake to righteousness, and sin not" (I Corinthians 15:34). In other words, God's way of changing us is to make us righteous on the inside and allow that righteousness to absorb us, spirit, soul, and body. This only happens as we become skillful in "the word of righteousness" (Hebrews 5:13).

We cannot commit righteousness just as Jesus never committed any sin, yet He was made sin with our sin. In turn, we were made righteous with His righteousness. We were made the righteousness of God the moment we received Jesus as our Lord and Savior (2 Corinthians 5:21).

So every person who has ever made Jesus the Lord of their life has exactly the same righteous standing with God. God is righteous, and He is no respecter of persons.

What's more, if God demands that every person accept the sacrifice of Jesus or the shedding of Jesus' blood for the remission of their sin, then when someone accepts that sacrifice, God must accept that person as though sin never existed in their life.

Once we, as believers, get a good concept of that, then we will begin to realize that righteousness is not something we have. It's something we are. It's what we have become.

The last effect of righteousness from Isaiah 32:17 is quietness.

Quietness is the result of knowing that God will always do what His Word says He will. In Isaiah 55:11, God says, "So shall my word be that goeth forth out of my mouth: it shall not return unto me void, but is shall accomplish that which I please, and it shall prosper in the thing whereto I sent it." And in Jeremiah 1:12: "… I will hasten my word to perform it." Finally, 2 Peter 3:9 states, "The Lord is not slack concerning his promise, as some men count slackness; but is longsuffering to us-ward, not willing that any should perish, but that all should come to repentance."

Now let us look at an example of Jesus walking in His righteousness as an example of how God expects us to act:

> And when they drew nigh unto Jerusalem, and were come to Bethphage, unto the Mount of Olives, then sent Jesus two disciples,
>
> Saying unto them, Go into the village over against you, and straightway ye shall find an ass tied, and a colt with her: loose them, and bring them unto me.
>
> And if any man say ought unto you ye shall say, The Lord hath need of them; and straightway he will send them. (Matthew 21:1–3)

Here we see Jesus sending His disciples to go to a specific place where they would find a young colt to bring back so He could ride it into Jerusalem. How did Jesus know all that, even down to the fact that it never been ridden before? God told Him!

Remember, too, that God is righteous. Jesus was depending on God being right in this situation, just as He had depended on God's rightness in every situation up to that time. That, I believe, is why Jesus also told His disciples, "The son can do nothing of himself, but what he seeth the Father do" (John 5:19, 8:29.

God told Jesus about the donkey, and the disciples found everything to be just as Jesus told them.

You might say, "Yeah, but that was Jesus." But for us to get where Jesus wants us to be, we have to understand that what happened was the righteousness of God in and on Jesus, just as it is in and on every believer at this very moment. The difference is faith in that righteousness.

Another example happened before Jesus' crucifixion when He sent His disciples to find the right room in which to celebrate the Passover feast. There is no indication that Jesus spent any time wondering where they would celebrate Passover or how they would pay for the feast (Matthew 25:18; Mark 14:13–14; Luke 22:10-11).

No. The righteousness of God in Jesus was moving out in front of Him providing for His needs all of the time. And because of that, Jesus was able to walk in total assurance and quietness through it all.

And that is where you and I can live today. All we have to do is press into and become conscious of the reality of the righteousness God birthed in us the moment we received Jesus as Lord and Savior. And as that consciousness of righteousness grows and develops within us, it will eventually become bigger and more powerful than all the problems that surround us.

In Genesis 15:6, we see that Abraham "believed in the Lord; and he counted it to him for righteousness." In other words, God dealt with him as though he had not sinned. We are also the righteousness of God, and the blood of Jesus cleanses us from all sin—if we believe God.

Faith is the key. The key is not in feeling guilty or allowing condemnation of any kind. The key is knowing who you are in Christ!

A righteous man is not absolutely perfect but is a person who is doing good things, listening to God, and knowing that his prayers are being answered. If he misses it, he has only to sincerely say, "Jesus, I'm sorry. I have messed up and sinned; please forgive me," and the blood of Jesus comes in like a flood to wipe the slate clean!

Confess: I am the righteousness of God in Christ Jesus. I have a right to all the blessings that are in the Kingdom of God. I have been raised up to sit with Christ in Heavenly places and all of those things belong to me.

YOUR BUILDING BLOCKS FOR LIFE

Your words are building blocks from which you can construct your life and future. With your words, you can set the cornerstones of your life, and they will allow you to live within the confines of that boundary that you have created or move you into an unlimited realm. Situations, circumstances, and conditions are all subject to change, but with the support of your words, you can establish them in your life forever.

Your words will create an image on the inside of you that will take you wherever you want to go, and the Word of God has that ability to do so.

The following verses are a good example of this, for your words based on God's Word are vital to your health and well being:

(Proverbs 18:21): Death and life are in the power of the tongue: and they that love it shall eat the fruit thereof .

(Luke 6:45): A good man out of the good treasure of his heart bringeth forth that which is good; and an evil man out of the evil treasure of his heart bringeth forth that which is evil: for of the abundance of the heart his mouth speaketh.

(Job 22:28): Thou shalt also decree a thing, and it shall be established unto thee: and the light shall shine upon thy ways.

(Proverbs 18:7) A fool's mouth is his destruction, and his lips are the snare of his soul .

Mark 11:23): For verily I say unto you, That whosoever shall say unto this mountain, Be thou removed, and be thou cast into the sea; and shall not doubt in his heart, but shall believe that those things which he saith shall come to pass; he shall have whatsoever he saith .

(Proverbs 16:9): A man's heart deviseth his way: but the Lord directeth his steps.

(Proverbs 18:20-21): A man's belly shall be satisfied with the fruit of his mouth; and with the increase of his lips shall he be filled.

Death and life are in the power of the tongue: and they that love it shall eat the fruit thereof .

(James 3:6): … the tongue is a fire, a world of iniquity: so is the tongue among our members, that it defileth the whole body, and setteth on fire the course of nature; and it is set on fire of hell .

(Proverbs 21:23): Whoso keepeth his mouth and his tongue keepeth his soul from troubles .

(Isaiah 57:19): I create the fruit of the lips; Peace, peace to him that is far off, and to him that is near, saith the Lord; and I will heal him .

(Proverbs 10:11): The mouth of a righteous man is a well of life.

(Proverbs 12:6): … the mouth of the upright shall deliver them .

A man shall be satisfied with good by the fruit of his mouth (Proverbs 12:14).

(Proverbs 12:18): … the tongue of the wise is health.

(Proverbs 13:3 NKJ): He that guards his mouth keepeth his life).

(Proverbs 14:3): … the lips of the wise shall preserve them.

(Proverbs 15:4): A wholesome tongue is a tree of life: but perverseness therein is a breach in the spirit.

(Proverbs 15:4 AMP): A gentle tongue [with its healing power] is a tree of life, but willful contrariness in it breaks down the spirit.

(Proverbs 15:2 NKJ): The tongue of the wise useth knowledge rightly, but the mouth of fools pours forth foolishness .

(Proverbs 16:23): The heart of the wise teacheth his mouth, and addeth learning to his lips .

(Proverbs 16:24): Pleasant words are as an honeycomb, sweet to the soul and health to the bones .

As you meditate on the above verses, it is important for you to notice that your words have the ability to turn your life in the direction that you choose it to go.

You can change your destiny by changing your thoughts and the words that you speak.

Your thoughts often become your words.

Your words become your actions.

Your actions become your habits.

Your habits become your character.

Your character becomes your destiny or what you are now.

You take a thought by saying it. Matthew 6:31 tells us to "…take no thought saying." If you desire to have or possess a thought, your first step is to think about it, and your second step is to say it. You do it over and over until it becomes a habit. Then you will get to the point that when something happens, suddenly those words will come out of your mouth without you even thinking about it.

II Corinthians 13:5 (AMP) instructs to "Examine and test and evaluate your own selves to see whether you are holding to your faith and showing the proper fruits of it. Test and prove yourselves [not Christ]." So start taking notice of what you are saying, looking at, and hearing. If you will stay in faith and get rid of negative, harmful thoughts, God will take what the devil meant for your harm and turn it around for your good and use it to your advantage. Romans 8:6–8 AMP tells us, "Now the mind of the flesh [which is sense and reason without the Holy Spirit] is death [death that comprises all the miseries arising from sin, both here and hereafter]. But the mind of the [Holy] Spirit is life and [soul] peace [both now and forever]. [That is] because the mind of the flesh [with its carnal thoughts and purposes] is hostile to God, for it does not submit itself to God's Law; indeed it cannot. So then those who are living the life of the flesh [catering to the appetites and impulses of their carnal nature] cannot please or satisfy God, or be acceptable to Him."

Luke 6:45 says, "A good man out of the good treasure of his heart bringeth forth that which is good; and an evil man out of the evil treasure of his heart bringeth forth that which is evil: for of the abundance of the heart his mouth speaketh."

What is in abundance in your heart? Is it good or is it evil? You only have to listen to your words when something happens and you don't have time to think about what you are going to say.

If you don't like what you are hearing, you can make a change by thinking on and speaking out God's Word. You can overcome the world, the flesh, and the devil by the blood of the Lamb and the word of your testimony. As you give voice to the law of the Spirit of life in Christ Jesus, it makes you free from the law of sin and death, and you now have the choice to not allow sin, sickness, or death to lord it over you. Remember, it is when you give voice to God's Word that the law of the Spirit of life in Christ Jesus is able to make you free from the law of sin and death (Romans 6:13–14, 8:2; I John 4:4, 5:18; Revelation 12:11).

It's your choice! Ask yourself: What am I doing to show that Jesus is the Lord of my life? Am I still living the same life that I lived before I accepted Jesus into my life, or am I renewing my mind with the Word of God and making myself acceptable to be used by God as His ambassador here on the earth?

Is God FIRST in your life? In your *F*inances, *I*nterests, *R*elationships, *S*chedule, and *T*roubles? If you can say that God is first in these five areas of your life, then it is a pretty good sign that God is first in all of your life. If not, you need to get into the Word of God and find out which areas need working on.

Joshua 1:8 says, "This book of the law shall not depart out of thy mouth, but thou shalt meditate therein day and night, that thou mayest observe to do according to all that is written therein; for then shall thou make thy way prosperous, and then thou shalt have good success."

The *thy* and *thou* in this verse is you. It is up to you to determine how much you will prosper and have good success in your walk with God. God's limits are for you to be blessed "exceeding abundantly above all that you can ask or think" (Ephesians 3:20). And your goal should be to experience the: "exceeding greatness of His power to us-word who believe according to the working of His mighty power. Which he wrought in Christ, when he raised him from the dead, and set him at his own right hand in the heavenly places" (Ephesians 1:19-20).

Jesus has instructed us in Matthew22:37: "Thou shalt love the Lord thy God with all thy heart, and with all thy soul, and with all thy mind." And in Romans 8:6-7 we are told, "To be carnally minded is death; but to be spiritually minded is life and peace. Because the carnal mind is enmity against God" for it is not subject to the law of God, neither indeed can be." And in I Peter 1:13 and I Corinthians 2:16 (NIV), we are told to "… prepare our mind for action, because …we have the mind of Christ."

The choice is yours! Nobody can make it for you. You can be all that you can be in Christ, or you can be just who you are.

8

FAITH WILL NOT WORK WITH BITTERNESS, RESENTFULNESS, AND UNFORGIVENESS IN YOUR HEART

And when you stand praying, forgive, if you have ought against any: that your father also which is in heaven may forgive you your trespasses. (Mark 11:25)

If there is a spirit of bitterness, resentfulness, or unforgiveness about you, your faith will not work, and your prayers will not be answered. If your faith and your prayers are not working for you, I believe that this is the first place for you to look.

As a born-again Christian, you are free from unforgiveness and strife. You are compelled to forgive others as Christ has forgiven you, for the love of God is shed abroad in your heart by the Holy Ghost (Matthew 6:12; Romans 5:5, 6:11).

Make it a point in your life to never be offended by what others say about or do to you (Mark 4:17). Those people are not your problem. What they say or do is between them and God, and what you say or do is between you and God.

The Word says in Ephesians 6:12: "For we wrestle not against flesh and blood, but against principalities, against powers, against the rulers of the darkness of this world, against spiritual wickedness in high places."

Those people that say or do those things are not the problem, but the devils and demonic spirits that are influencing them are. In John 10:10, we are told that "The thief cometh not, but for to steal, and to kill, and to destroy."

The thief is the devil, and he is influencing them and is doing everything that you will allow him to do to destroy your life and your relationship with God.

On the other hand, "You are God's workmanship, created in Christ Jesus unto good works, which God hath before ordained that you should walk in them" (Ephesians 2:10), and "You are complete in Him [in Christ], which is the head of all principality and power (Colossians 2:10).

Jesus has given unto us power [authority] to tread on serpents and scorpions, and over all the power of the enemy: and [if you use your authority properly] nothing shall by any means hurt you. (Luke 10:19) [Emphasis added by author].

Jesus has not only given us authority over the devil and his crowd but He has provided us with all of the weapons that we will ever have need of. To top it off, II Corinthians 10:4 tells us, "For the weapons of our warfare are not carnal, but mighty through God to the pulling down of strong holds".

And in Matthew 18:18 Jesus said: "I will give unto thee the keys of the kingdom of heaven and whatsoever ye shall bind on earth shall be bound in heaven: and whatsoever ye shall loose on earth shall be loosed in heaven."

To *bind*, from the Greek *deoo*, is to bind, tie, fasten, paralyze, to render totally helpless, to declare unlawful. To *loose* is from the Greek *luoo*, meaning to break the grip, or paralyze the grip, cause to release.

Matthew 6:33 (AMP) tells us that the Kingdom of God and his righteousness are: "His way of doing and being right." And Luke 17:20–21 tells us: "The kingdom of God cometh not with observation: For, behold, the kingdom of God is within you."

Jesus said, "My kingdom doesn't come with observation." It is God's way of doing and being right, and it is within men. You and me, the born-again children of God are able to operate on the same level of faith with God because we are joint-heirs with Christ (Romans 8:17): "And if ye be Christ's, then are ye Abraham's seed, and heirs according to the promise" (Galatians 3:29).

What promise? The promise that the Holy Spirit made to Abraham: that his seed would possess the gate of his enemies.

The Amplified Bible gives us Matthew 16:19 this way: "And I will give unto thee the keys of the kingdom of heaven: and whatever you bind (declare to be improper and unlawful) on earth must be what is already bound in heaven; and whatever you loose (declare lawful) on earth must be what is already loosed in heaven."

Jesus is telling us here that He will give believers authority and power to loose things on earth that are allowed in heaven and to bind things on earth that are not allowed in heaven.

Do you know what things won't be found in heaven? There is no sickness or disease in heaven, and there is no poverty. There is no evil, no lack of any kind, and no unhappiness.

Jesus is telling us that we have authority to bind the evil forces upon earth that cause sickness, disease, poverty, and sin.

What is loosed in heaven? Life, health, abundance, happiness, joy, and peace! This should make it easier to understand why Jesus called the power of binding and loosing the keys of the kingdom of God.

You can clearly see from the above scriptures that God has given you power and authority, and it is up to you to do something about devils and those demon spirits who have planted bitterness and unbelief in your heart. It is up to you to kick the devil out of your territory and refuse defeat. You enforce the Word of God in your life and refuse to back off until you have the victory that belongs to you. Although the devil may try to discourage you and plant doubt in your heart about God's promises, you can make a quality decision to guard your heart and mouth and refuse to speak defeat (Colossians 2:6–7; Romans 4:21).

Read Matthew 4:1–11 to see an example on how Jesus dealt with the devil. That same principle is available to you and will work every time. Simply tell the devil that "it is written" and quote the appropriate scripture that applies to him. James 4:7 tells us to: "Resist the devil, and he will flee from you." That is a promise from God to you: if you do the resisting, the devil will do the fleeing, as if in fear! The devil lives in terrible fear of anyone who knows and uses their power and authority that they have in Christ.

In Luke 17:1–6, Jesus taught His disciple about bitterness and unforgiveness and about how to remove these evil forces from one's life. Jesus compared these forces to the sycamine tree that was so well known in that part of the world. The word *sycamine* comes from the *Greek sukamino* and refers to a tree that grew throughout the Middle East. To understand all that is connected to the sycamine tree, you will know why Jesus used this tree as an example of bitterness and unforgiveness. In Luke 17:6, Jesus told His disciples: "… If ye had faith as a grain of mustard seed, ye might say unto this sycamine tree. Be thou plucked up by the root, and be thou planted in the sea; and it should obey you." Notice that Jesus said, "Ye might say unto this sycamine tree." The word *this* indicates that Jesus was pointing out something specific to them.

The sycamine tree was known to have one of the deepest root structures of all the trees in the Middle East. It was a fast growing tree and often grew to a height of thirty feet or more, and with its large root structure, it was very difficult to kill because of its tremendous root system in which the roots went deep and were spread over a large area.

The same is with bitterness and unforgiveness in that they must be dealt with in such a manner that all of the root system is destroyed to keep it from resurfacing in another place.

The roots of bitterness and unforgiveness go deep down into the human soul, and they are fed by any offense that lies hidden in the soil of the heart. If one does not make a serious decision to rip out those roots of bitterness and offense and get them out of his heart once and for all, even the littlest offense will often cause these evil forces to grow and spring up in his life.

Back in Luke 17:3, Jesus instructed His disciples that they needed to forgive those who had sinned against them. He then instructed them in verse 4 by saying that even if a brother does something wrong seven times in a day and each time is truly repentant, they were to keep on forgiving the offending brother. To forgive only once is often a challenge to many people. But to forgive more than once in the same day is almost impossible.

The disciples must have thought that Jesus was somewhat pushing the limits, because in verse 5 they said, "Lord, increase our faith." I believe that they were saying, "Lord, we don't know if we have enough faith to forgive so many times in one day. You'll just have to increase our faith if we're going to do it seven times in one day!"

Jesus then took the opportunity to teach the disciples how to get all bitterness and unforgiveness out of their lives by telling them that bitterness, resentfulness, and unforgiveness are just like that sycamine tree. If you really want to be free of these attitudes, you can speak to that menacing growth in your life and command it to be pulled up by the roots and planted into the sea (Mark 11:23).

Just like the sycamine tree, bitterness, resentfulness, and unforgiveness are very fast growing, and if not controlled, they will start taking over the whole place. When you allow those ugly attitudes to grow freely, they will not only spoil the condition of your heart by killing your joy, spoiling your peace, and canceling your spiritual life, but they will ruin your relationships with other people.

The fruit of the sycamine tree is very bitter and was only eaten by the poorer people. In fact, it was so bitter that it couldn't be eaten whole but had to be mixed with other food and nibbled on over a period of time to make it digestible.

Just like the fruit of the sycamine tree, the fruits of bitterness, resentfulness, and unforgiveness are bitter, tart, and pungent. Those people who are bitter and filled with unforgiveness chew on their feelings for a long time. They nibble on it for a while, then they pause to digest it, and after a while, they take another bite to think and meditate on the offense, stirring up their bitter feelings toward those who have offended them. In the end, their continuous nibbling on the bitter fruit makes them bitter, sour people themselves.

The poor people were the majority consumers of the sycamine fruit and as such, those who sit around and constantly meditate on every wrong thing that has ever been done to them are usually bound up with all kinds of poverty. Their bitter attitude makes them spiritually poor, but they are also frequently defeated, depressed, sick, and financially poor as well.

Jesus said in Luke 17:6 that in order to rid ourselves of this nuisance of bitterness from our lives, we must have faith the size of "a grain of mustard seed." The word *grain* is the Greek word *kokkos*. It describes a seed, grain, or very small kernel. And the word *mustard* is the Greek word *sinapi*, which refers to the small mustard plant that grows from a tiny, miniscule seed.

Jesus is explaining to us here that a great amount of faith is not needed to deal with the bitterness, resentfulness, and unforgiveness in our lives. Any person who has even a tiny measure of faith can speak to bitterness and unforgiveness and command them to leave if that is the desire of his heart. Again, it is your choice.

When you decide to deal with the wrong attitudes that you have been dealing with in your life, you must order them to "be thou plucked up by the root, and be thou planted in the sea" (Luke 17:6).

The phrase "plucked up by the root" are from the Greek *ekridzoo*, which is a compound of the words *ek* and *ridzo*. The word *ek* means out, and the word *ridzo* is the Greek word for a root, like the roots of a plant. When they are joined into one word, the compound word means, to rip out by the roots.

This is referring to a person who is fully determined to grab that plant at the base by faith and pull with all of his might and jerk the roots right out of the ground, leaving no suckers behind to grow up later and produce life again. And once that you have ripped those attitudes out of the soil of your soul, mind, will, and emotions, Jesus said that you are to command them to "be planted in the sea." So we are to permanently relocate that nuisance, that mountain of bitterness and unforgiveness, in the sea. Because the sea is made up of salt water, the salt will kill the roots, preventing the plant from growing. Then, no matter how hard one tries to resurrect that plant, it will never grow again. It is a dead issue, and its life is dead forever!

Once you have followed Jesus' directions and commanded bitterness and unforgiveness to leave, don't ever allow them to take root in your life again. Understand that your flesh will have moments when it would like nothing better than to dwell on those old hurts again, but don't ever allow it. You must bury it in the sea of forgetfulness so that its roots can never regain a foothold in your soul.

Jesus told us to say to the sycamine tree, "Be thou plucked up by the root, be thou planted in the sea; and it should obey you." Did you notice that last phrase? "and it shall obey you." The word *obey* is the Greek word *huakouo,* which means to submit to and obey.

Jesus specifically said that you must literally speak to the sycamine tree. The word *say* used here is from the Greek *lego,* which means to speak, but the tense that is used depicts a strong, stern, serious, deeply felt kind of speaking. In other words, this is not a person who mutters thoughtless nonsense. This is a person who has meditated this Word and is convinced that what he says will happen. He boldly speaks authoritatively and with great conviction, because he knows that his voice represents his authority.

When you make that choice to rise up and speak to your emotions and exert your authority in Jesus Christ, your flesh will obey your commands. If you don't take authority over and speak to your emotions, they will take authority over you and speak to you. If you don't rise up and conquer your flesh, it will rise up and conquer you. It is time for you to do the talking and to take command of your thought life by not letting your emotions tell you what to think, what to do, or how to react.

Remember, you are a spirit-being that has been created in the likeness and image of God. God is a spirit (John 4:24). You are a spirit-being; you have a soul which consists of your mind, will, and emotions; and you live in a body (I Thessalonians 5:23).

9

YOUR FAITH MUST BE RELEASED BY WORDS FROM YOUR MOUTH

You can have faith and never release that faith!

> That whosoever shall *say* unto this mountain, Be thou removed, and be thou cast into the sea; and shall not doubt in his heart, but shall believe that those things which he *saith* shall come to pass; he shall have whatsoever he *saith*. (Mark 11:23)

Notice that in this verse the words *say* or *saith* are used four times, and the word *believe* is only there once. You don't get a revelation of the Bible with your head; you have to get a revelation of it with your heart. And that revelation comes after you have spoken the Word over and over several times.

Most Christians are missing God's best in their prayers, because they don't say what they believe. You probably have been taught to believe, but chances are you have not been taught that your faith must be released by your words. And those words must say what you can have when you say it, because you are required to believe it in your heart. How do you get that belief down into your heart? By hearing the Word of God concerning those things that you are believing God for. Those things which he saith are words. Whatsoever he saith are words. It is the words that you hear that increase your faith and you are going to have what you say. So if you are not getting what you are believing God for, you need to take an inventory of what you have been saying.

All that you have and all that you are is the result of what you have been saying. Take the time to inventory what you have and what you are and compare it to what you have been saying. You might be surprised at what you find.

Your words are building blocks from which you can construct your life and future. With your words you can set the cornerstones of your life, which will allow you to live within the confines of the boundary that you have created or move you into the realm of unlimited possibilities.

Situations, circumstances, and conditions are all subject to change, and with the support of your words, you can establish them in your life forever. Your words will create an image on the inside of you that will take you wherever you want to go, and the Word of God has the ability within itself to do so.

The following verses are a good example of this, because words based on God's Word are vital to your health and well being:

> (Luke 6:45): A good man out of the good treasure of his heart bringeth forth that which is good; and an evil man out of the evil treasure of his heart bringeth forth that which is evil: for of the abundance of the heart his mouth speaketh.
>
> (Job 22:28): Thou shalt also decree a thing, and it shall be established unto thee: and the light shall shine upon thy ways.
>
> (Proverbs 18:7): A fool's mouth is his destruction, and his lips are the snare of his soul.
>
> (Mark 11:23): For verily I say unto you, That whosoever shall say unto this mountain, Be thou removed, and be thou cast into the sea; and shall not doubt in his heart, but shall believe that those things which he saith shall come to pass; he shall have whatsoever he saith.
>
> (Proverbs 16:9): A man's heart deviseth his way: but the Lord directeth his steps.
>
> (Proverbs 18-21): A man's belly shall be satisfied with the fruit of his mouth; and with the increase of his lips shall he be filled.
>
> Death and life are in the power of the tongue: and they that love it shall eat the fruit thereof.
>
> (James 3:6): … the tongue is a fire, a world of iniquity: so is the tongue among our members, that it defileth the whole body, and setteth on fire the course of nature; and it is set on fire of hell.

(Proverbs 21:23): Whoso keepeth his mouth and his tongue keepeth his soul from troubles.

(Isaiah 57:19): I create the fruit of the lips; Peace, peace to him that is far off, and to him that is near, saith the Lord; and I will heal him.

(Proverbs 10:11): The mouth of a righteous man is a well of life.

(Proverbs 12:6): … the mouth of the upright shall deliver them.

(Proverbs 12:14): A man shall be satisfied with good by the fruit of his mouth.

(Proverbs 12:18): … the tongue of the wise is health.

(Proverbs 13:3): He that keepeth his mouth keepeth his life.

(Proverbs 14:3): … the lips of the wise shall preserve them.

(Proverbs 15:4): A wholesome tongue is a tree of life: but perverseness therein is a breach in the spirit.

(Proverbs 15:4 AMP): A gentle tongue [with its healing power] is a tree of life, but willful contrariness in it breaks down the spirit.

Proverbs 15:2): The tongue of the wise useth knowledge aright: but the mouth of fools poureth out foolishness.

(Proverbs 16:23-24): The heart of the wise teacheth his mouth, and addeth learning to his lips

Pleasant words are as an honeycomb, sweet to the soul, and health to the bones.

As you meditate on the above verses, it is important for you to notice that your words have the ability to turn your life in the direction that you choose it to go. Proverbs 6:2 (AMP) tells us that: "You are snared [taken captive] with the words of your lips; you are caught by the speech of your mouth" [Emphasis added by author].

What God is saying here is that your words dominate your life. The devil has gotten a lot of blame for things that people have caused by the words of their mouths. You were snared, or taken captive, by the words of your mouth. You shall have whatsoever you say, so never talk failure or defeat. Never confess that God's power cannot put you over the top. You need to become God inside of you minded. I John 4:4 tells us that: "Greater is He that is in me than he that he that is in the world," and in Galatians 2:20, we are told that "Christ liveth in me."

Confess: I believe that He, the Christ that lives in me, is greater than all of my tests and trials, all of the problems that I could be facing, and all of the circumstances that seem to have me bound. He is greater than anything that could come against me. And I make the decision now to always speak words that are based on the Word of God to direct my life in the direction that God wants it to go.

Who or what is this Christ? Christ is the Greek word *kris-tos*, which means Messiah. *Messiah* is the Hebrew word for anointed. Christ translated into English means the Anointed One.

What is "The Anointed One" doing in you? Do you ever recognize His presence? Do you realize that He is in there to strengthen you, comfort you, and help you through life? I can assure you that He is in there to take you over the top and experience victory in every area of your life.

That anointing is the burden removing, yoke destroying power of God and is available to everyone who believes and that anointing is there to help you in your everyday life. It doesn't make any difference whether you are a housewife or the CEO of a large corporation. That anointing is there to assist you to be the very best that you can be. (Isaiah 10:27)

Everything will happen that God said will happen if you will believe it and confess it. Learn to use words that will work for you, positive faith filled words, and acknowledge that God is God. He is the greater one who lives in you, and you can have whatsoever you say because, Jesus said that He would never leave you nor forsake you (II Corinthians 2:14; Philippians 4:13; Hebrews 13:5).

To give you a good example, when Israel came up out of Egypt, they camped at a place called Kadesh-barnea, and Moses sent twelve spies out to the land of Canaan. When they returned, all but two of them had an evil report. Now, an evil report is a report of doubt and unbelief (Numbers 13:17–33).

Caleb and Joshua came back and said, "Let us go up at once, and possess it; for we are well able to overcome it" (verse 30). But the other ten said, "We be not able to go up against the people; for they are stronger than we." And they got exactly what they confessed. They brought back an evil report filled with doubt and unbelief, and they all died out in the wilderness except for Caleb and Joshua (verse 31).

In Joshua 14:7–9, we see Joshua speaking:

> Forty years old was I when Moses the servant of the Lord sent me from Kadesh-barnea to spy out the land; and I brought him word again as it was in mine heart.
>
> Nevertheless my brethren that went up with me made the heart of the people melt: but I wholly followed the Lord my God.
>
> And Moses sware on that day, saying, surely the land whereon thy feet have trodden shall be thine inheritance, and thy children are for ever, because thou hast wholly followed the Lord my God.

Caleb and Joshua said, "we are well able to overcome it, for the Lord is with us, we can do it, and we can take the land." The ten died out there in the wilderness, and Joshua and Caleb lived to enter the promise land because of their positive confession.

Now when you are facing the giants in your life, don't have a negative confession and don't have an evil report; faith always has a positive report. Don't talk about what you are not able to do but always talk about what God can do through you. A believer has absolutely no business talking doubt and unbelief, because both of these things are of the devil. In fact, a Christian has no business hanging around other Christians or non-Christians who are talking doubt and unbelief. Before you know it, they will drag you down to their level. (Psalms 1:1-2)

To experience God's strength in your life, you must know that "The joy of the Lord is your strength" (Nehemiah 8:10). I just can't emphasize enough to you that you need to take an inventory of what words are coming out of your mouth. You must choose your words carefully, because those words can make your life happy, or they can make your life miserable. Your words can drag you down, or your words can lift you up. James 3:8 tells us that the tongue is "full of deadly poison," and verse 10 tells us that "from the same mouth comes blessings and cursing."

With your tongue you can bless your life, or you can curse your life. Your words can bring you joy, peace, happiness, and victory or defeat and discouragement. James 3:4–5 instructs us to: "Look at the ships also, though they are so great and are driven by strong winds, are still directed by a very small rudder wherever the inclination of the pilot desires. So also the tongue is a small part of the body, and yet it boasts of great things."

If you have lost your joy, the first thing that you need to do is take an inventory of just what you have been saying about yourself, about your circumstances, and about your future. Human nature turns to murmuring and complaining when things get tough. The more that you talk about your problems, the more depressed you will become the longer that you will stay in that depressed situation.

God's Word says nothing about us talking about our pain and suffering. That is a trick of the devil.

Changing the way that you talk can bring joy into your life. Words are like seeds—they have creative power, and when you speak something out, you are giving life to what you are saying, either good or bad. And every time that you repeat it, it is just like you are putting water and fertilizer on that seed, and it will eventually produce what you are prophesying. If you are always talking about your problems, murmuring, and complaining, you will always experience that defeat. If you are saying that nothing good ever happens to you, nothing good will ever happen to you, and if you are talking about taking the flu or a cold, you will soon be experiencing the first symptoms.

You need to stop talking about the problem and start talking about the solution. Stop speaking words of defeat and instead start speaking words of victory. Don't use your words to describe your situation; instead, use your words to change your situation. God's Word tells us in Joel 3:10 to "Let the weak say, I am strong"—or, let the troubled say I am free. It is up to you to get your words lined up with the Word of God; you can't just say what you want or what you feel or what you think, but you must say what God says about you. You must say positive things that line up with the Word of God.

Say things like, "I shall not die but live and declare the works of the Lord. With long life is God satisfying me and showing me my salvation. I am strong in the Lord and the power of His might. No weapon that is formed against me shall prosper, and nothing shall by any means hurt me, nor any accident overtake me, for God always causes me to triumph." (Psalms 118:17, 91:12, 16; Ephesians 6:10; Isaiah 54:17; II Corinthians 2:14).

You have to speak the victory before you will ever see the victory. It is not enough for you to believe God's Word; you must give life to your faith by speaking it out. You can change the world around you by changing your words.

Proverbs 18:21 tells us that "Death and life are in the power of your tongue." So when you use your words the right way, they will bring you joy and victory, but when you use your words the wrong way, they will bring you discouragement and failure. You can't have a negative tongue and expect to live a positive life. But if you choose to have a negative mouth, you are going to have a negative life. It is never acceptable to say negative or critical things about yourself, and it is just as wrong to criticize yourself as it is to criticize another person. Thinking and speaking negative things about yourself and others is a trick of the devil designed to destroy your life and keep you down below the level that God wants you to reside at!

You have been made in the image and likeness of almighty God (Genesis 1:26–27; James 3:9), and when you are criticizing yourself, you are criticizing God's very best. You are saying, "God, You didn't do a very good job when you made me." No, God did not make a mistake with you; He did not make a failure. Don't let another negative word come out of your mouth about yourself. You may not be perfect; you may have a lot of faults, failures, and shortcomings, because everybody does. Stop being so hard on yourself, because negative words will poison your future. The words that you speak go out of your mouth, and they come right back into your ears. Remember, faith comes by hearing. And if you hear those words long enough, they will drop down into your spirit, and you will become just what you are saying. That is why it is so important for you to only say good things about yourself. Instead of confessing what you can't do, you should start declaring: "I can do all things through Christ who strengthens me. The favor of God surrounds me like a shield, and everything that I touch prospers. The blessings of God are chasing me down and overtaking me. I just can't outrun the good things of God."

You can prophesy your future, because your words have creative power. Quit talking about how bad life is treating you, what you don't have, and what you can't do. Instead, if you will start speaking words of faith and victory, things will begin to change in your life, and you will experience the joy of the Lord.

Let's take some time here to study Israel's journey out of Egypt and how they talked and what their negative confession cost them.

In Deuteronomy 6:3, God talks about the Promised Land that He had given to the children of Israel. God miraculously delivered them out of Egypt and led them through the Red Sea toward that Promised Land. However, when confronted with the harshness of the desert on the other side of the sea, the children of Israel forgot the promises God had given them and chose to live in their problem, literally.

Instead of facing the task head on and walking straight through the desert, they groaned and complained to God and began to sin and rebel. (Does that sound familiar?) What could have taken them days turned into a forty-year journey. They walked around the same mountain for more than half a generation, making no progress in getting to their destination.

Similarly, Christians today often confuse motion with progress. We repeat the same problem again and again, mistakenly convincing ourselves that we are making progress in the right direction. Yet, in reality, we are stagnating, walking in circles around the same issues every day. If you do not overcome your problems, they will overcome you, and you will die in them and never reach the destination that God has intended for you. That is why God says in Hosea 4:6, "My people are destroyed for a lack of knowledge."

The devil knows that empty heads are much easier to deceive. That's why he loves it when he finds a believer who makes no effort to fill his mind and heart with the truth from the Word of God. The devil knows it when he has found another empty head and can't wait to fill it with his lies and bring it under his control. Are you one of those or do you know someone who is?

Who or what is going to control your mind? Are you going to allow God and His Word or the devil and his lies? Your mind is going to be filled with something, and you now have the opportunity to choose the right thing to fill it. Your choice in the matter will determine your success or your failure in life, so make sure you make the choice wisely. (Isaiah 26:3 AMP)

In times of difficulty, you will find that you have to guard your tongue more than ever and carefully choose the words that you speak, because your words are either going to make or break you. Proverbs 6:2 tells us that, "Thou are snared by the words of your mouth."

The word *snare* means to trap or capture, ensnare. Again this is a good time to take an inventory of the words that are coming out of your mouth and judge them as to whether they are positive encouraging words that will build you up, or are they negative words that will tear you down?

In III John 2, Paul is praying for you saying that he wishes above all things that you may prosper and be in health, even as your soul prospers. Remember that your soul consists of your mind, will, and emotions.

One of God's most fervent desires is for you to prosper in your soul. This means that He wants you to mature spiritually and be full-grown in your mind, your will, and your emotions. He wants you to think with the "mind of Christ" (I Corinthians 2:16) and according to His Word. When you are able to do that, you can separate your emotions from the decisions that you need to make and use your will to line up your life with God's will for you. And to the degree that you are able to do that, He also wants you to prosper and be healthy in all areas of your life (Psalms 35:27).

But so many times we get to looking at the circumstances and let our negative words tie the hands of almighty God. God works by faith. Jesus said, if you can, all things are possible (Mark 9:23 NIV). You have to be a believer and act on your faith, because "faith without works is dead". (James 2:26).

How often do we get a promise in God's Word, and then when we get into a little difficulty, we start giving into doubt and unbelief instead of standing and acting on God's Word? Next we find ourselves studying the situation and sizing up our opponent, and if we are not careful, we will do just like the children of Israel did; we will start murmuring and complaining and speaking negative words. And when we hear and act upon those negative words, we open up the door to the devil. So the best thing that you can do in a situation like this is to start speaking God's Word that pertains to your situation. If you can't do that, the next best for you to do is keep your mouth shut and practice the vocabulary of silence.

Ephesians 4:29 tells us to "let no corrupt communication proceed out of your mouth." In other words, if you can't say something good about yourself, others, or the situation you are facing, just zip your lips and don't say anything at all. Silence is better than speaking those negative, unfruitful words of lack and defeat which will make your life that much more difficult.

God knows the power of our words, and He works by laws. If you go around murmuring and complaining and always speaking negative destructive words, you are tying the hands of almighty God. Your tongue is going to control your life. James 3:4 tells us that just as a tiny little rudder controls the direction of a huge ship, so the tongue will set and control the direction of your life. If you have a negative tongue, you are going to have a negative life.

You can have negative circumstances, but if you will have a positive tongue, then you can have a positive life in the midst of negative circumstances. Your tongue sets the direction for your life not your circumstances. In I Peter 3:10 (AMP), the Word says, "For let him who wants to enjoy life and see good days [good—whether apparent or not] keep his tongue free from evil and his lips from guile (treachery, deceit)."

When it says evil, it's not talking just about when we say negative, hurtful things toward other people, but it is when we murmur and complain or when we have a negative report. Your tongue or your words are what set the direction for your life. Which direction are you going? Are you blessing your life or cursing it? Are you magnifying God or your problems? Are you making yourself miserable because of your words or uplifting your life with words of praise and worship?

Take note of I Peter 3:12 where we are told that "the eyes of the Lord are upon the righteous (those who are upright and in right standing with God), and His ears are attentive to their prayer. But the face of the Lord is against those who practice evil [to oppose them, to frustrate, and defeat them]." (Psalm 34:12-16) When you have a problem, the more that you talk about that problem, the more upset that you are going to become. The more you talk about something, the more you magnify it or make it bigger than it really is. When you are always talking about the negative things in your life, those negative words are going to cause you to lose your joy, which will cause you stay down and discouraged.

When you became a Christian, you inherited the joy of the Lord right down on the inside of you. But the reason that we seldom experience that joy is because we poisoned our joy with our negative words. You can start enjoying your life right now if you simply stop poisoning your soul by murmuring and complaining. Change the direction of your life by starting each day with a good confession of faith. The following is one example:

"Good morning, Lord Jesus. For this day I again declare that You are my Lord (referring to Your majesty, honor, authority, and sovereignty). I submit this day and all that it contains to You. For this is the day which the Lord has made; I will rejoice and be glad in it, for the joy of the Lord is my strength. I am strong in you, Lord, and the power of Your might, and I can do all things through Christ who strengthens me. For You, Lord, are at work in me, creating in me the power and the desire, both to will and to work for Your good pleasure" (Romans 10:9; Psalms 27:14, 118:24; Nehemiah 8:10; Ephesians 6:10; Philippians 4:13, 2:13).

In John 16:22, Jesus tells us not to allow anyone to steal our joy, because in Nehemiah 8:10 we are told that "the joy of the Lord is your strength." Your spiritual strength is the power source for the anointing. Holding on to your joy is a decision that you will have to make each and every day. You need to make it a habit to wake up every morning and make the above confession, and you must be determined not to allow circumstances, sickness, trouble, or other people to rob your joy. When you learn how to keep your life full of joy, God will be there, and He will work in your life. That's His grace in action; His power and ability extended to you.

Instead of complaining, just thank God by faith for what you have and who you are in Christ. When you change your perspective and speak the right words, you will have joy in the midst of your difficulties. Ephesians 5:18 tells us to continually be filled with the Holy Spirit, which is an ongoing process, and Ephesians 5:19 tells us that we are to stay full of the Holy Spirit by speaking to ourselves in psalms and hymns, by singing and making melody in our hearts to the Lord, and by constantly giving God thanks. In short, we should be constantly giving God praises and thanks for all that He is doing for us based on the words of faith that we are speaking (Psalms 118:24).

Here is a good example to get you started:

"I thank You, Lord, that I am strong and healthy. I thank You that I am able to be your ambassador here on the earth, and I thank You for equipping me with Your Name and the power of Your Word so that Your light may shine before men, that they may see Your good works and be drawn to you" (I Peter 2:24; II Corinthians 5:20; Matthew 5:16).

With every step that you take, you should be giving praise to God, because He knows the power of your words. In Romans 4:17, we see where Abraham "... called things that be not as though they were." By using that same principle in a positive way instead of complaining and bringing in more misery, more trouble, more heartache, more pain, more defeat, and more discouragement, you create a pathway for God to work in your life. With your words, you are setting the direction for your life.

Take control of your tongue, because you can prophesy your future by speaking words of victory in Christ Jesus. You must stop talking words of defeat about how bad things are and start talking about how blessed you are; stop talking poverty and start talking prosperity.

You must declare the vision for your life; you have to speak out the direction that God has placed in your heart. Not only do you have to hear it, but God and the enemy need to hear it also.

Jesus tells us in Matthew 23:12 and Luke 14:11, 18:14 that "those that exalt themselves will be brought down." And Peter instructs us in I Peter 5:6 to "Humble yourselves therefore under the mighty hand of God that he may exalt you in due time."

Change takes place when you're thankful and not critical. Do not complain; your situation may not look all that good, but don't complain about it. I Thessalonians 5:18 (AMP) says, "Thank [God] in everything [no matter what the circumstances may be, be thankful and give thanks], for this is the will of God for you [who are] in Christ Jesus [the Revealer and Mediator of that will]." (Colossians 2:7 AMP) If you want God's best, you must do what God's Word says. Ephesians 6:10 encourages us to "Finally, my brethren, be strong in the Lord and in the power of his might." Here Paul is giving us some very important insight into the kind of power that God has made available to you and me. It is the kind of power that God wants to use to operate through us to fight with unseen, demonic powers that come to war against the soul.

The word *strong*, from the word *endunamao*, describes a power whose purpose is to infuse a believer with an excessive dose of inward strength. This type of *endunamao* power is strong enough to withstand any attack and successfully oppose any kind of demonic force.

The word *power*, from the Greek *kratos*, describes a demonstrated power—a power that is demonstrative, eruptive, and tangible and usually comes with some type of an external, outward manifestation of real power that one can actually see.

The word might, from the word *ischuos*, depicts a very strong person with great muscular capabilities.

Notice that we are to be strong in the Lord and in the power of His might. The words *power* and *might* are describing God, one who is able, mighty, and muscular.

You might ask where this powerful, mighty ability of God is working today. If we will allow it, it is in you and me!

Ephesians 1:20 tells us that God "raised him [Jesus] from the dead, and set him at his own right hand in the heavenly places." And in Ephesians 2:6, we are told that God "raised us up together, and made us sit together in heavenly places in Christ Jesus."

If we are seated with Christ, and Christ is seated next to God the Father in heaven, then we are seated next to God the Father in heaven also. And if God raised Jesus "far above all principality, and power, and might, and dominion, and every name that is named, not only in this world, but also in that which is to come: And hath put all things under his feet, and have him to be the head over all things to the church" (Ephesians 1:21–22), this means that whatever Jesus received from the Father becomes yours as well. All that you have to do is believe it and receive it by faith because you are a joint-heir with Christ (Romans 8:17; II Timothy 3:15–17; Mark 11:24; Colossians 2:12).

The next time you run into a problem that seems a little over-whelming, remind yourself that "… greater is he that is in me than he that is in the world" (I John 4:4). You have the greater One living on the inside of you, and you have no need to be afraid and no need to shrink back in timidity, for there is enough power at work in you to resist any force that would come against you and to supernaturally remedy any situation that needs to be changed.

The Bible depicts Jesus after His resurrection as seated in heavenly places at the right hand of God. Being seated refers to being in the rest of God. God wants each one of us to enter into His rest; our part is to believe and rest in Him, and His part is to work on our behalf. Physically, we are on the earth, but simultaneously we are spiritually seated with Him in heaven. Everything that God the Father provided for Jesus to accomplish His assignment here on this earth and all that Jesus provided for us at the cross is available for us to use in our assignment to be ambassadors to Christ here on the earth. When we first do our part, He will always do His part!

I encourage you to be assured in your faith that God will follow through with what He has promised you in His word. Get His promises into your mind, meditate on them, speak them out loud, and let your faith increase (Ephesians 1:20, 2:6; Romans 10:19; Hebrews 4:9– 11, Joshua 1:8; II Corinthians 5:20).

Every day you need to praise God and confess that: Greater is He that is in me than he that is in the world. I am more than a conquer, and I can do all things through Christ who strengthens me. I am the head and not the tail, and I am well able to fulfill my destiny.

The more that you say it, the more those words are going to get on the inside of you, the more your faith is going to be built up, and the more you will have that vision of victory for your life (Romans 8:37; Philippians 4:13; Deuteronomy 28:44).

You are not just quoting words, but you are prophesying your future. Once you start saying it and seeing it, nothing will be able to stop you from receiving it. That is faith in action, and that is what gets God's attention. And God will move heaven and earth to bring it to pass (I Peter 3:10).

10

TALKING TO YOUR MOUNTAIN

And Jesus answering said unto them, Have faith in God.
[Or have the God-kind of faith.]

For verily I say unto you. That whosoever shall *say* unto
this mountain, Be thou removed, and be thou cast into the
sea; and shall not doubt in his heart, but shall believe that
those things which he *saith* shall come to pass; he shall have
whatsoever he *saith*.

Therefore I say unto you, what things soever you desire,
when you pray, believe that you receive them and you shall
have them

And when you stand praying, forgive, if you have aught
against any: that your Father also which is in heaven may
forgive you your trespasses.

But if you do not forgive, neither will your Father which
is in heaven forgive your trespasses. (Mark 11:22–26)

In verse 23, "That whosoever shall say unto this mountain," is referring
to the mountains in your life. That mountain may be debt, sickness,
unemployment, or any assortment of problems that have crept up in your
life. Mark 11:23–26 teaches us how to deal with these mountains and move
them out of your life.

Notice that in verse 23 the words *pray* and *prayer* are not there, but the
word *say* is, and in verse 24, the word *pray* is there. Faith will work by saying
it without praying for it (verse 23). Faith will also work with prayer (verse 24),
but when you pray it, you have to say it. In both instances, you will hear the
words that you are saying. Romans: 10:17 says that "faith cometh by hearing,

and hearing by the word of God." So whether you say it or pray it, your faith is being increased as you hear the Word of God spoken.

Hebrews 10:23 instructs us to "hold fast the profession [confession] of our faith without wavering." Don't ever give up. When you are in need of something, you only need to confess that you have it: "… but shall believe that those things which he saith shall come to pass; he shall have whatsoever he saith." Or you can pray for it and get it: "What things soever you desire, when you pray, believe that you receive them, and you shall have them." (Mark 11:23-24). In both methods, you have to exercise your faith and believe God for what you need. You may have to say it only once, but chances are you will have to say it several times a day for days, weeks, or sometimes even months. It is when it gets down in your heart that you will see the manifestation of what you are believing for. But if you don't give up, it will materialize. God is faithful; you do your part, and He will do His (I Corinthians 1:9; I Thessalonians 5:24).

God's word is God's will, and it is God's will that you exercise your faith to get your needs met. Philippians 4:19 tells us, "But my God shall supply all your need according to his riches in glory by Christ Jesus." Now we know from the first chapter of John that Jesus and the Word of God are one and the same, and in the above verse, we see that it is God's will that we have our need supplied to us according to his riches in glory by Christ Jesus or by applying the Word of God in our lives.

God's will for you is found in III John 2: "Beloved, I wish above all things that thou may prosper and be in health, even as your soul prospers." Here we can see that it is God's will that we have prosperity materially, physically, and spiritually.

God accomplishes almost everything on the earth by the principle of seed time and harvest. In my experience, anytime that I have gone to the Father with a request, I have found that His first reaction is for me to plant a seed following the Kingdom of God principles, which when kept properly watered with the Word of God and tended properly with my faith, produces the desired harvest. Every seed has a name, and when it is planted, that is the crop that is harvested. In essence, when you plant a seed into the Kingdom of God, it is your responsibility to put a name on that seed to get a harvest of the desired results.

God is a faith God, and without faith, it is impossible to please Him (Hebrews 11:6). Isaiah 1:19 says, "If you are willing and obedient, you shall eat the good of the land." You must be willing to do God's will and be obedient to follow God's instructions to get your need met. And when you do you, will experience God doing things that are "exceeding abundantly above all that we ask or think, according to the power that worketh in us." And that power that works in you is your faith! (Ephesians 3:20)

There are some things that God just does not have to give us. Money and material needs are good examples; like faith, just where would He get them? He can't make them, because that would be counterfeiting. They are already here on this earth, and it's our faith that will get them from where they are into our hands. Those things belong to us, but it is up to us to exercise our faith and cause God to work for us. Philippians 4:19 tells us that "My God shall supply all of your need according to His riches in glory by Christ Jesus."

The key is to know how to get God to supply that need. Psalms 115:16 tells us that "The heaven, even the heavens, are the Lord's: but the earth hath he given to the children of men." Everything on this planet and every resource in it belongs to us. We don't have to ask God for it, because He has already given it to us. But if you don't claim ownership of it, the devil will steal it from you.

God made everything that is in this earth, and he didn't make it for the devil and his crowd (Psalms 24:1). "The earth is the Lord's, and the fullness thereof." It is His because He is the creator, and He made it for His man Adam, to whom He gave dominion over it all (Genesis 1:29). But Adam refused to take ownership of what God had given to him. Adam was the original god of this world, but he didn't do his job and instead committed high treason and sold out to Satan, allowing him to become the god of this world (II Corinthians 4:4).

This all happened because Adam refused to deal with what belonged to him. Adam was to keep and dress the garden. God gave him dominion over all the works of His hand; in short, he had the authority to rule it as he chose to, except for the tree of life (Genesis 2:15–17, 3:11). That tree was God's, and Adam had explicit instructions to leave it alone.

Because of Adam's transgression, Satan is now dominating the whole thing. But Jesus came and redeemed us from the hand of the enemy. We now have the authority to claim anything that we need and we now have the authority to command the devil and his demon spirits to take their hands off of those things that we are in need of (I Corinthians 15:22–45; Matthew 18:18).

It all comes about by saying it. Faith works by saying it without praying, but it also works by praying. When you pray, believe that you will receive it. There is just a shade of difference between saying it and praying it. You can't just believe it; you have to say just what it is that you are believing for. You must believe that those things that you say shall come to pass. Just keep saying and believing that those things shall come to pass, and sooner or later, you shall have what you say.

Confess: I believe that I receive; I believe that I receive; I believe that I receive, and I shall have it! The believing comes first and then the receiving. I must release my faith to see the manifestation of what I am believing God for! When I hook my faith to the power of God I will see results!

As a believer, you must meditate on the Word and envision yourself with what God's Word says that you can have, even though you don't see it out there yet. You have to dream it before you will receive it! The Word of God never profits unless it is mixed with faith in them that hear it.

Whenever you hear the Word of God, Satan will come immediately and try to steal it from your heart. He is only successful when you don't understand what you have heard, because faith refuses to be moved in the face of affliction and persecution. The only way to rid fear from your life is to resist the devil and walk in the love of God, as perfect love casts out fear.

Mark 4:14–15 says:

The sower soweth the word.

And these are they by the wayside, where the word is sown; but when they have heard, Satan cometh immediately, and taketh away the word that was sown in their hearts.

And how does he do it? Verses17 and 19 tell us:

When affliction or persecution ariseth for the word's sake, immediately they are offended....

And the cares of this world, and the deceitfulness of riches, and the lusts of other things entering in, choke the word, and it becomes unfruitful.

These verses reveal the devil's method of operation. They show us that as soon as the seed of God's Word is planted in your heart, the devil starts working to get rid of it. He starts trying to dig it up before it has a chance to take root.

Did you notice the tools the devil uses to achieve this? The tools of affliction or persecution, the cares of the world, the deceitfulness of riches, and the lusts (pressures) of other things (II Timothy 3:12; Mark 10:29).

Affliction and persecution are nothing more than the devil trying to get your mind off of the Word of God and an expression of Satan's terrible fear of all born-again Christians. He sends a person along to offend you by saying something mean to hurt your feelings or gets someone to irritate and provoke you until you step over into strife.

Note: The word *devil* in the Greek carries the idea of a constant irritation, poking, pressing, or pecking away at something in order to penetrate and get entrance into it, and the word *offense* is defined as the name of the part of a trap to which the bait is attached, hence, the trap or snare itself.

We don't think of offense as being bait or the center of the trap, but once you allow offense to attach itself to your heart, it will stop the power of God from flowing into your life. This is why we all need to protect the spiritual condition of our hearts.

It is so important that you don't become offended by what other people are saying or allow the problems of this world, the deceitfulness of riches, and the pressures of other things to enter into your life to choke the word and cause it to be unfruitful. Make a quality decision that you are going to stay in the Word and believe God until you see the manifestation of what you are believing God for.

Then take a few minutes several times a day praising God for who He is and what He is doing for you. Praise is the highest form of prayer, because God inhabits the praise of His people (Psalms 22:3). When you spend time praising God, joy comes up in your spirit, that joy of the Lord becomes your strength, you become strong in the Lord and the power of His might, and then you can do all things through Christ who strengthens you. That is why Jesus was able to say in John 14:12: "the works that I do shall he do also; and greater works than these shall he do, because I go unto my Father." (Ephesians 6:10; Nehemiah 8:10) You put action to your faith, and the Christ in you will do the work!

11

YOUR FAITH WILL ALWAYS WORK FOR YOU

Have faith in God.

For verily I say unto you, That whosoever shall say unto this mountain, Be thou removed, and be thou cast into the sea; and shall not doubt in his heart, but shall believe that those things which he saith shall come to pass; he shall have whatsoever he saith.

Therefore I say unto you, what things soever you desire when you pray, believe that you receive them, and you shall have them.

And when you stand praying, forgive, if you have ought against any: that your Father also which is in heaven may forgive your trespasses.

But if you do not forgive, neither will your Father which is in heaven forgive your trespasses. (Mark 11:22–26)

Notice the number of times that the word *you* is used in these verses. What is it telling you? It tells me that God is talking to me, instructing me, and teaching me how to have and walk in that God-kind of faith.

Now God is no respecter of persons (Acts 10:34). He is the same yesterday, today, and forever (Hebrews 13:8). And faith, the God-kind of faith, will work the same for you as it does for me. You received a measure of faith when you invited Jesus Christ into your life as your Lord and Savior, and now it is up to you to build that faith up by hearing the Word of God and exercising what faith you now have.

It is so important that you read carefully and notice in verses 23 and 24 the words *he, his,* and *you.*

> For verily I say unto *you,* That whosoever shall say unto this mountain, Be thou removed, and be thou cast into the sea; and shall not doubt in *his* heart, but shall believe that those things which *he* saith shall come to pass; *he* shall have whatsoever *he* saith.
>
> What things soever *you* desire, when *you* pray, *you* believe that *you* receive them, and *you* shall have them.

For the most part, *you* have to do it. You have to do the believing. I can't do it for you; your uncle Joe can't do it for you; your aunt Betty can't do it for you. You have to do it yourself. You can't push your desires over on somebody else, and other people can't push their desires over on you. You can get your desires by exercising your faith, but you cannot extend your desires into other people's lives.

According to Matthew 18:19, "That if two of you shall agree on earth as touching any thing that they shall ask, it shall be done for them of my Father which is in heaven." So, based on that scripture, if you can get somebody else to agree with you in faith, then you can get your desire and their desire to be in agreement and get the job done. The important thing to note here is that the two must be in agreement on what they are asking for (Amos 3:3). One cannot be saying in his heart that he believes something will happen while the other is saying that he hopes it happens. Both parties must know and understand just what the other person is praying and believing God for and be in total agreement that God will act just that way. There is never any agreement when one person is hoping and the other is believing, and God will never answer a prayer under those circumstances.

I personally believe that most of the time when people go forward for prayer in the churches, they don't get their healing because both parties are not in agreement.

> And he said unto them, Go you into all the world, and preach the gospel to every creature.
>
> He that believeth and is baptized shall be saved; but he that believeth not shall be damned.
>
> And these signs shall follow them that believe; in my name shall they cast out devils; they shall speak with new tongues;

> They shall take up serpents; and if they drink any deadly
> thing, it shall not hurt them; they shall lay hands on the
> sick, and they shall recover. (Mark 16:15–18)

In some instances, when dealing with nonbelievers or new Christians, a mature Christian will be able to carry the day and see healing manifested with his own faith. As long as people are new Christians or those who know nothing about God's way of doing things, you can carry them with your faith and get things done. But people who have heard the Word and have seen the Word in operation are expected to get their needs met on their own faith.

So release your faith for God's protection by confessing Psalms 91:

> [I am] He that dwelleth in the secret place of the most High,
> and I shall abide under the shadow of the Almighty.
> I say of You, Lord, You are my refuge and my fortress:
> My God; in You do I put my trust.
> Surely You have delivered me from the snare of the
> fowler and from the noisome pestilence.
> You are covering me with your feathers and under Your
> wings do I place my trust: for Your Word is my shield and
> my buckler.
> I am not afraid of the terror by night, nor of the arrow
> that flieth by day,
> Nor of the pestilence that walketh in darkness, nor of
> the destruction that wasteth at noonday.
> A thousand shall fall at my side, and ten thousand at my
> right hand, but it shall not come near me.
> Only with my eyes shall I behold and see the reward of
> the wicked.
> Because I have made You Lord, which is my refuge, even
> the most High, my habitation;
> There shall no accident come near me, neither shall any
> plague come near my dwelling.
> For You, Lord, have given Your angels charge over me to
> keep me in all my ways.
> They are bearing me up in their hands, lest I dash my
> foot against a stone.
> I shall tread upon the lion and adder: the young lion
> and the dragon shalt I trample under my feet.

Because I have set my love upon You, Lord, You have delivered me: You have set me on high, because I know Your Name.

Whenever I call upon You, You always answer me: You are with me in my troubles: You have delivered me, and honored me.

With a long life are You satisfying me and showing me my salvation. [Author's interpretation]

Faith is not just words, but it is what you believe. It is what is in the abundance of your heart that will carry the day for you in a time of trouble. True faith is a fight. You wager warfare, and having done all to stand, you stand on God's Word. You don't look for an excuse to give up. Giving up is not an option. You must continue until you have what you are believing God for.

Hebrews 11:6 tells us that "Without faith you cannot please God." So when you are exercising your faith, you are pleasing Him, and He takes great delight in it. And when you "Delight yourself in the Lord, and He shall give thee the desire of thine heart" (Psalms 31:4).

By faith we believe that God is in control no matter what we are experiencing. We have often made mistakes that God will be forced to work through. We have planted seeds in our lives and have watered them with our negative words, and those crops will either have to be pulled up by the roots or otherwise disposed of before God can do His work in your life.

God has given us His shoulder to lean on, and when you lean on Him, you can depend on His grace to kick in and carry the day. God's grace is God's power and ability extended to us. But it takes your faith to activate it!

12

Exercising Your Faith

You can make your life whatever you want it to be by exercising you faith. Two examples of this are found in Luke 8:41–56:

> And behold, there came a man named Jairus, and he was a ruler of the synagogue: and he fell down at Jesus' feet, and besought him that he would come into his house:
>
> For he had one only daughter, about twelve years of age, and she lay a dying. But as he went the people thronged him.
>
> And a woman having an issue of blood twelve years, which had spent all her living upon physicians, neither could be healed of any,
>
> Came behind him, and touched the border of his garment: and immediately her issue of blood stanched.
>
> And Jesus said, Who touched me? When all denied, Peter and they that were with him said, Master, the multitude throng thee and press thee, and sayest thou, Who touched me?
>
> And Jesus said, somebody hath touched me: for I perceive that virtue is gone out of me.
>
> And when the woman saw that she was not hid, she came trembling, and falling down before him, she declared unto him before all the people for what cause she had touched him, and how she was healed immediately.
>
> And he said unto her, Daughter, be of good comfort: thy faith hath made thee whole; go in peace.

While he yet spake, there cometh one from the ruler of the synagogue's house, saying to him, Thy daughter is dead; trouble not the Master.

But when Jesus heard it, he answered him saying, Fear not: believe only, and she shall be made whole.

And when he came into the house, he suffered no man to go in, save Peter, and James, and John, and the father and the mother of the maiden.

And all wept, and bewailed her: but he said, Weep not; she is not dead, but sleepeth.

And they laughed him to scorn, knowing that she was dead.

And he put them all out, and took her by the hand, and called, saying, Maid, arise.

And her spirit came again, and she arose straightway: and he commanded to give her meat.

And her parents were astonished: but he charged them that they should tell no man what was done. (Matthew 9:18–26; Mark 5:21–43)

Two important things to note are that Jairus was a ruler of the synagogue and a high official in the local church, and by this time the rulers and high officials in the church were strongly opposed to Jesus and his teachings. So much so, that plans were being made to kill him.

But being filled with anxiety over his only daughter's nearing death, Jairus willingly joined the multitude waiting for Jesus who was just returning from the country of the Gadarenes. Yet Jairus was willing to press through the crowd and fall to his knees and beg a favor from Jesus, the very man his peers were planning to kill.

Next we have a woman, who was diseased with an issue of blood for twelve years. In her religious tradition, a woman with an issue of blood was considered in the same category as a leper. She was not supposed to mingle in public. If anyone came close to her, she was to cry, "Unclean! Unclean!" The women in Israel at that time did not have the same rights and privileges to mix freely in public that most women in the world now have. The law dictated that she be killed for coming out in public in this condition. Yet she had the tenacity to be persistent enough to act on her faith and push her way through the crowd and touch the hem of Jesus' garment, which put a demand on God's power through her faith, and she was made whole because of it. She didn't let public sentiment and her own religious teachings stand between her and getting to Jesus.

Notice the four steps this woman used in getting her desire:

1. She said it. "For she said, If I may touch but his closes, I shall be whole" (Mark 5:28).

    Positive or negative, according to what you say, that is what you shall receive. This woman had the opportunity to make a negative statement instead of a positive one. There are lots of negative things that she could have expounded upon, based on her experiences, and that is what she would have received. But she made a positive statement. If I may touch but his clothes, I shall be whole—and it came to pass. What she kept saying was her faith speaking!

    The woman hoped to be healed as she pressed through the crowd. The Amplified Bible says: "For she kept saying, if I only touch His garments, I shall be restored to health." Notice, she kept saying it over and over; "... if I only touch His garments, I shall be restored to health."

    She was filling her hope with a faith image. She set her own point of contact to receive her healing. Her words penetrated her spirit, and she began to see herself well. As she kept making that confession of faith, she was filling her hope with a faith image so that "grow worse" image of despair and defeat had to give way to the faith-filled words that came from her own mouth.

2. She did it. She got into the very midst of the crowd, which was not an easy thing to accomplish, as the crowd was packed in around him, and she reached through to touch Jesus' clothes. When she did, she put a demand on God's power to heal her.

    "For as the body without the spirit is dead, so faith without works is dead also" (James 2:26). It wouldn't have done this woman any good to have said: "If I may but touch His clothes, I shall be whole," and not act on what she said. Her actions were her faith speaking! When she touched His clothes, her touch of faith made a demand on the covenant of God and the anointing that was upon Jesus.

    What she was saying was her faith talking, and when she acted out what she said and touched His garment, that faith that was in her became the substance of her hope, and her words became a living reality. Your actions will either put you over, or they will defeat you. Your actions either allow you to receive from God or they keep you from receiving from God.

3. She received it. "What things soever you desire, when you pray, believe that you receive them, and you shall have them" (Mark 11:24). Jesus knew that power had gone out of Him. At that time, Jesus was the only representative of the Godhead at work upon the earth. He was anointed of God with the Holy Spirit (Acts 10:38).

    Her faith gave substance to and brought about the manifestation of healing that was already hers because of the covenant. But she had to call for it.

    In that day, to get to where the power was, you had to go where Jesus was. Now, under the new covenant, we have the Holy Spirit in the person of the Godhead at work upon the earth, and we have direct access to Him because we are in Christ, and He lives in us (Romans 8:11; John 6:63; I Corinthians 3:16).

4. She told it. When Jesus perceived that virtue (that healing power of God) had gone out of Him, He asked: "Who touched me?

    "And when the woman saw that she was not hid, she came trembling, and falling down before him, she declared unto him before all the people for what cause she had touched him, and how she was healed immediately" (Luke 8:46–47).

    In the same manner, if someone lays hands on you in faith based on the Word from Mark 16:18, it is your responsibility to give praise to God for what He has done and tell others that God has healed you no matter what it looks like. To do otherwise is to refuse to allow the manifestation of your healing to materialize. Remember, "Faith is the substance of things hoped for, the evidence of things not seen." You exercise your faith based on what the Word of God says and not on what you can see. You call things that be not as though they were, not as they are! (Hebrews 11:1; Romans 4:17).

    Tell it so that others may know how you gave voice to God's Word so that they may also believe it and receive it. That is how you can write your own ticket to victory over the world, the flesh, and the devil (I John 4:4; Revelation 12:11).

You must train yourself to speak God's Word. Ephesians 5:1 (AMP) directs us to: "Therefore be imitators of God [copy Him and follow His example], as well-beloved children [imitate their father]."

We are to imitate God as a child does his father. We are faith children of a faith God, and we should act like God. If a child imitates his father, he will walk like him, talk like him, and pattern his every move like him. As so, as children of God, we should do no less after our Father, God.

Jesus gave us examples, and we should take note that He: (1) Spent much time in prayer, but He never prayed the problem but always prayed the answer. His words always were in alignment with what God had already said. (2) He always spoke accurately, never crooked speech. His words were always in line to what God had said. (3) He always spoke the end results, not the problem. Take notice that throughout the Gospels Jesus never confessed present circumstances. He only spoke the desired results. (4) He always used the written Word to defeat the devil. (It is written.)

Look at and meditate on the following verses and see how they can set the groundwork for your confessions of faith:

Mark 9:23: "All things are possible to them that believe …"

Luke 17:6: "… if you had faith as a seed you should say."

John 3:36: "… he that believeth hath …"

Mark 11:23–24: "… whosoever shall say … he shall have …"

Isaiah 54:17: "No weapon [of Satan] that is formed against thee [me] shall prosper …" (notes added by the author)

Luke 10:19: "… nothing shall by any means hurt you [me]."

Psalms 91:10: "There shall no evil befall me, neither shall any plague come nigh my dwelling."

It is the Bible principle of believing and calling for things that are not yet manifest. The Word of God conceived in your heart, formed by your tongue, and spoken out of your mouth is creative power.

God declares in Isaiah 55:11 that His Word will not return to Him void, and we are to return it to Him by giving voice to it.

Giving voice to your faith in God's Word is what is going to get your needs met. Every time you speak out in faith, it creates a stronger image on the inside of you. Whatever your desire is, the image of you having it will be created by God's Word and your continual affirmation and agreement with it. Eventually, that image will be perfected by the Word of God, and you will begin to see yourself with your need met. When God's Word is engrafted into you, it infuses its life into you, and your victory is the result (John 6:63; Romans 8:11).

Jesus said, "If ye abide in me, and my words abide in you, ye shall ask what ye will, and it shall be done unto you" (John 15:7).

When God's Word becomes engrafted or infused into your spirit, it has become a part of you, and it cannot be separated from you. It is not only your thought and affirmation, it is you. It's the Word made flesh. Then your flesh will reflect the life of your need. When God's Word concerning that need takes root in your flesh, it will become greater than the problem, and the end result will be your victory.

The image that the Word of God creates in you is already a reality in the spirit realm. When you speak God's Word from your heart, your faith gives substance to the promises of God. Jesus made it plain in Matthew 12:35: "a good man out of the good treasure of his heart brings forth good things."

As you study the first chapter of Genesis, you will notice that every time God spoke, creation took place because words are the carriers of faith. "The worlds were framed by the word of God," and "it was good" (Hebrews 11:3; Genesis 1:10, 12, 18, 21, 25, 31). Without words, there wouldn't have been any creation. Your words create images, and eventually you will live out the reality of that image.

You giving voice to God's Word enables the law of the Spirit of life in Christ Jesus to break you free from the law of sin and death, enabling you to overcome the world, the flesh, and the devil (Romans 8:1–2; I John 4:4; Revelation 12:11).

When the messenger came, Jairus' heart probably sank like a rock in water because he was thinking: "My daughter is dying right now! This woman has had her problem for twelve years, and she can wait a little longer, but my daughter can't." But Jesus, immediately upon hearing the bad report from the messenger, chose to not be affected by it. He spoke up before Jairus was able to speak out a negative report.

The devil will also use the same tactic on us whenever he finds an opportunity to do so. When one thinks that things can't get any worse, a negative report seems to always come our way telling us that things are getting worse. This is why no matter what we see or hear, we must keep our attention focused on what the Word of God says about the situation and not let our minds be led off to the negative side where we will speak out a negative report. A good example of this is found in Matthew 14: 23–32 (AMP):

> And after He [Jesus] had dismissed the multitudes, He went up into the hills by Himself to pray. When it was evening, He was still there alone.

But the boat was by this time out on the sea, many furlongs [a furlong is one-eighth of a mile] distant from the land, beaten and tossed by the waves, for the wind was against them.

And in the forth watch [between 3:00–6:00 AM] of the night, Jesus came to them, walking on the sea.

And when the disciples saw Him walking on the sea, they were terrified and said, It is a ghost! And they screamed out with fright.

But instantly He spoke to them, saying, Take courage! I Am! Stop being afraid! (Exodus 3:14) And Peter answered Him, Lord, if it is You, command me to come to You on the water.

He said, Come! So Peter got out of the boat and walked on the water, and he came toward Jesus.

But when he perceived and felt the strong wind, he was frightened, and as he began to sink, he called out, Lord, save me [from death]!

Instantly Jesus reached out His hand and caught and held him, saying to him, O you of little faith, why did you doubt?

And when they got into the boat, the wind ceased.

Peter perceived and felt the strong wind because he did not keep his eyes on Jesus. He allowed what he perceived to frighten him, and from that, he made a negative confession based on that fear.

It was miraculous that Peter walked on the water for a short distance, but he still missed out on God's best. We know that because Jesus rebuked Peter instead of commending him for the distance he did walk on the water saying, "O thou of little faith, wherefore didst thou doubt" (verse 31).

Peter's doubt robbed him and everyone who was present of a greater blessing. God's best was for Peter to walk to Jesus and for the two of them to return to the ship together.

We don't have any right to criticize Peter for his lack of faith until we can prove that we can walk on water. Peter actually did walk on the water and made it close enough to Jesus to allow Him to reach out and catch him as he was sinking.

Peter was able to walk on the water because he believed what Jesus said. He acted on one word: "come" (verse 29). On that single word, Peter jumped out of the boat onto a rough sea and began to walk toward Jesus. And as long as he continued acting on Jesus' Word, he continued walking.

We see that Peter began to sink "when he saw the wind boisterous" (verse 30). He made a mistake by taking his eyes off of Jesus and focusing on the strong wind and the rough waves. And at the moment Peter became afraid, he began to sink. He quit walking by faith and began walking by sight.

Notice that Jesus was so full of faith that He was able to reach out and grab Peter's hand and help him back into the boat.

Jesus also knew that Jairus' daughter would live and be made whole regardless of the present circumstances, and He told Jairus not to fear but only to believe, and his daughter would be made whole.

Fear is faith working in reverse (or *false evidence that appears real*), and faith believes what God said is true. That is what Jairus would need to see his daughter alive and well.

Jesus would allow only Peter, James, John, and the parents into the house with Him and the dead girl, which leaves some questions, because it is easy to speculate that there were others trying to get in. Would their lack of faith have a difference? We see that the mourning crowd were mocking and laughing at Jesus for claiming that the girl was only sleeping. They knew that Jairus' daughter was dead. It had to have taken some time for the messenger to come from the home, get through the crowd that thronged Jesus, and deliver the message and then for them to return to the home. Yet, notice that Jesus was not affected by the message of the girl's death, the fear in Jairus, the angry disciples who were not allowed into the home, or the mocking mourners. Jesus simply refused to be affected by what the world was doing or saying around Him.

As such, when we have a problem, a mountain in front of us, we are to put our focus on Jesus, the Word, and not allow doubt and unbelief to crowd in around us and smother out our faith.

We should never deny the existence of a mountain in our lives, but we can deny it's authority to stay and refuse to allow it to stop the plan that God has for our lives. We must never allow ourselves to be affected by the world's message. We must always allow our spirit to take precedents over the situation, because the spirit is much more powerful than the physical body or anything in the natural. The body can't live without the spirit, but the spirit can live without the body (Luke 8:55; James 2:26).

That's why Jesus made it clear to Jairus that even if He was late getting to his home, the girl would be made whole. And to be "whole" she would have to be alive and kicking. She wouldn't stay dead, no matter what the messenger said about the situation.

Matthew 9:21 says this about the lady with the issue of blood: "For she said within herself, if I may but touch his garment, I shall be whole." Notice that she took a thought and said within herself that if she would only touch Jesus' garment, she would be made whole, and then she acted upon it with the results that Jesus said in Matthew 9:22: "Daughter, be of good comfort; thy faith hath made thee whole."

So when you get a negative report, do not allow the message to come in and steal your faith. Remember that your spirit is stronger than your body, and God has promised you that if you would walk in love you will not die but live and declare the works of God and with long life will He satisfy you and show you your salvation (Psalms 91:16, 118:17).

Your faith will also make you whole, so fear not but only believe.

After Jesus was able to get the crowd out of the house, He "took the young girl by the hand: and called, saying, 'Maid, arise.' And her spirit came again, and she arose straightway: and he commanded to give her meat. And her parents were astonished: but he charged them that they should tell no man what was done."

Take notice that Jesus was not interested in the spectacular. He charged the parents not to tell anyone. He was not interested in having any publicity; He was interested "in doing good and healing all those that were oppressed of the devil" (Acts 10:38). And He tells us in John 14:10 that He wasn't the one doing the healing: "But the Father that dwelleth in me, he doeth the works" (I John 4:16).

Matthew 4:7 – 10 gives us in insight into how we will be tempted by the devil if we choose to accept the great commission that Jesus gave to the church in Mark 16:15.

There are three things that we are warned not to do: (1) Never use the Word of God for a personal advantage, because it is going to work for you anyway. (2) Never associate yourself with wicked people even for the attainment of your goal. (3) Never perform a godly act in a prideful spirit.

Jesus set the example and was able to do this because He had faith in God. He was not a spectator concerning His Father. He didn't have to draw God in from the distant regions of speculation, because He knew His Father.

Mark 11:22 tells us to "Have faith in God." You must have faith in God before you can have the faith of God or faith toward God. To have faith in God you must know God, not just know about Him. Religion teaches you about Him but very seldom teaches you or shows you how to know God.

To know God is to love Him, for God is love, and God is light, and in him there is no darkness at all (I John 4:16, 1:5). To know God you must have fellowship with Him, because you cannot be saved and not have fellowship with Him. On the other hand, you can be saved and not know God.

To walk in faith you must know how God will act and how He will react because "without faith it is impossible to please him; for he that cometh to God must believe that he is, and that he is a rewarder of them that diligently seek him" (Hebrews 11:6). Faith in God is a dominate conviction concerning God, His being, His character, and His government. To know God's character you must study His names, because His names will speak to you concerning what He will do, and then you will begin to understand and get a complete picture of the Father.

Man's chief end and ultimate purpose is to know God, and this occurs through an unfolding revelation: "And this is life eternal, that they might know thee the only true God" (John 17:3).

THE NAMES AND THE NATURE OF GOD

How important is a name? Is it merely a means of recognition, or is it essential to our identity? Your name represents the qualities and characteristics that set you apart from everyone else, and those considerations are all a part of your identity.

God Almighty reveals Himself to us in these revelations of His name, which will bring us out of bondage and allow us to establish a new relationship with Him.

"In the beginning God created the heavens and the earth" (Genesis 1:1). God, from the Hebrew *Elohiym*, in the plural, Gods, which denotes three in one: Father, Son, and Holy Spirit.

"And God said, Let us make man in our image, after our likeness..." (Genesis 1:26).

These two verses form the basis for our belief in one God who is omnipotent; the almighty God who created the heavens and the earth and all that is within.

God Almighty reveals Himself to us in these twelve revelations of His name – one name, twelve revelations. Although these revelations were given years apart, they were recorded in perfect order by the inspiration of the Holy Spirit, and each defines with perfection the nature of an awesome God.

Elohim: My Creator (Genesis 1:1)
Jehovah: My Lord God, my father (Genesis 2:7)
El Shaddai: My Supplier (Genesis 17:1)*
Adonai: My Master and Lord (Genesis 18:3)

Jehovah-Jireh: My Provider (Genesis 22:14)
Jehovah-Rophe: My Healer (Exodus 15:26)
Jehovah-Nissi: My Banner and Victory (Exodus 17:15)
Jehovah-M'kaddesh: My Sanctifier (Leviticus 20:7–8)
Jehovah-Tsidkenu: My Righteousness (Jeremiah 23:5–6)
Jehovah-Shalom: My Peace (Judges 6:24)
Jehovah-Rohi: My Shepherd (Psalms 23:1)
Jehovah-Shammah: The Lord is there (Ezekiel 48:35)

*God is our El Shaddai. God our supplier; the God of might, nourishment, bounty, and blessings. The God of more than enough; the God who is able to reverse, override, prolong, and accelerate natural law.

We serve a God who is "able to do exceeding abundantly above all that we ask or think, according to the power that worketh in us" (Ephesians 3:20). That power is called faith, and it "worketh"! *Worketh* is from the Greek *energeoo*, meaning to be operative, be at work, put forth power.

THE ATTRIBUTES OF GOD

God the Father Is:
All-powerful (Jeremiah 32:17, 27)
All-knowing (I John 3:20)
Omnipresent (Psalms 139:7–12)
Faithful (I Corinthians 10:13)
Immutable (Psalms 102:27)
Impartial (I Peter 1:17).
Infinite (I Kings. 8:27)
Just (Psalms 89:14)
Life (Psalms 36:9)
Loving (I John 48)
Long-suffering (Exodus 34:6–7)
Merciful (Lamentations 3:22–23)
Perfect (Deuteronomy 32:4)
Truthful (Psalms 117:2)
Wise (Acts 15:18)

God is love (I John 4:8).
God is light (John 8:12; I John 1:5).
God is life (Amos 5:4).
God is a Spirit (John 4:24).

God is good (Psalms 106:1, 145:9).

JESUS, THE SON OF GOD:

"For unto us a child is born, unto us a son is given: and the government shall be his shoulder: and his name shall be called Wonderful, Counselor, The mighty God, The everlasting Father, The prince of Peace" (Isaiah 9:6).

Divine names and titles ascribed to Jesus prove that He is, by nature, divine and a member of the Godhead. In the Word of God Jesus is called,

Emmanuel (Matthew 1:23)

God (John 1:1).

Lord (Luke 19:34).

Lord of All (Acts 10:36).

Lord of Glory (I Corinthians 2:8).

Wonderful, Counselor, Mighty God, Everlasting Father, Prince of Peace (Isaiah 9:6, 7).

The Lord's Christ (Luke 2:26).

Son of God (Romans 1:4).

His Son (John 3:16-18).

God's Beloved Son (Matthew 3:17).

Only Begotten Son (John 1:18).

The Alpha and Omega, Beginning and the End, the First and the Last (Revelation 22:13).

The Lord (Acts 9:17).

Son of the Highest (Luke 1:32).

Bread of God (John 6:33).

Holy One of God (Mark 1:24).

The Holy Child Jesus (Acts 4:30).

King of kings and Lord of lords (Revelation 19:16).

Lord and Savior (II Peter 3:2).

Word of God (Revelation 19:13).

The Word of God declares that by inheritance Jesus was given the most excellent name in heaven, on earth, and the world to come.

It is more excellent than any name on the earth or in the heavens: "God, who at sundry times and in divers manners spake in time past unto the fathers by the prophets, Hath in these last days spoken unto us by his Son, whom he hath appointed heir of all things, by whom also he made the worlds. Who being the brightness of his glory, and the express image of his person, and upholding all things by the Word of his power, when he had by himself purged our sins, sat down on the right hand of the Majesty on high. Being made so much better than the angels, as he hath by inheritance obtained a more excellent name than they" (Hebrews 1: 1-4). (Philippians 2:5-10; Ephesians 1:17-21)

The following names/titles and traits will give you a better insight of who and what Jesus is to us.

Name/Title	Trait/Provision
A scepter (Numbers 24:16–17)	Authority
The captain of the hosts (Joshua 5:14)	Victory
The rock of my salvation (2 Samuel 22:47)	Defense
The lifter up of my head (Psalms 3:3)	Confidence
The headstone of the corner (Psalms 118:22)	Support
The lily of the valley (Song of Solomon 2:1)	Freshness
The rose of Sharon (Song of Solomon 2:1)	Freshness
The great light (Isaiah 9:2)	Guidance
A nail fastened in a sure place (Isaiah 22:22–23)	Security
A sure foundation (Isaiah 28:16)	Strength
A wall of fire (Zechariah 2:5)	Protection
A refiner and purifier (Malachi 3:3)	Growth
The bridegroom (Matthew 25:10)	Affection
The bread of life (John 6:35)	Nourishment
The way, truth, and life (John 14:6)	Purpose
The deliverer (Romans 11:26)	Liberation
The power of God (I Corinthians 1:24)	Stamina
The wisdom of God (I Corinthians 1:24)	Enlightenment
The Lord of glory (I Corinthians 2:7–8)	Majesty
A quickening spirit (I Corinthians 15:45)	Energy
The head of the body (Colossians 1:18)	Supervision
The Lord of peace (II Thessalonians 3:16)	Comfort
The brightness of His glory (Hebrews 1:3)	Ecstasy
The express image of His person (Hebrews 1:3)	Reality
The propitiation (I John 2:2)	Forgiveness
The alpha and the omega (Revelation 1:8)	Totality
The hidden manna (Revelation 2:17)	Provision
The amen (Revelation 3:14)	Finality
The lion of the tribe of Judah (Revelation 5:5)	Boldness
The word of God (Revelation 19:3)	Creativity

The bright and morning star (Revelation 22:16)   Awakening

If you have made Jesus your Lord and Savior, He is responsible for you before Almighty God. He is responsible for your daily welfare.

Psalms 35:27 tells us to "let them say continually, let the Lord be magnified, which hath pleasure in the prosperity of his servant." God takes great pleasure when you prosper! That means He desires you to be fully supplied with an abundant provision, or your every need met in abundance, that you may help Him establish His covenant (Deuteronomy 8:18; Ephesians 3:20). Remember, Jesus came that you might have life and have it more abundantly (John 10:10). That abundant life is yours, but you must receive it through the words that proceed from your mouth and allow it to flow throughout your life.

Religion tells us that God works in mysterious ways, but when you get to know Him, you will find that it is not true. God will always react just like His Word says that He will.

THE HOLY SPIRIT:

The Holy Spirit resides in us when we first come to Christ, as we read in Acts 2:38: "Then Peter said unto them, Repent, and be baptized every one of you in the name of Jesus Christ for the remission of sins, and ye shall receive the gift of the Holy Ghost. For the promise is unto you, and to your children, and to all that are afar off, even as many as the Lord our God shall call."

The Holy Spirit brings the presence and power of God into our lives to help us become overcoming victorious Christians that defeat the enemy wherever we go. II Corinthians 3:17 tells us, "Now the Lord is that Spirit: and where the Spirit of the Lord is, there is liberty."

The following titles give us insight into the duties and responsibilities of the holy Spirit.

Advocate (I John 2:1)
Comforter (John 14:16, 5:26, 16:7)
Guide (John 16:7)
Helper (Romans 8:26; Hebrews 13:6; Psalms 30:10)
Teacher (I Corinthians 2:9–16)
Witness (Romans 8:16)

Jesus said this about the Holy Spirit:
"He [Himself] will testify regarding Me" (John 15:26 AMP).

"… he will reprove the world of sin, and of righteousness, and of judgment" (John 16:8).

"… he will guide you into all truth" (John 16:13).

"… he will show you things to come" (John 16:13).

"… the love of God is shed abroad in our hearts by the Holy Ghost" (Romans 5:5).

"Now the Lord is the Spirit, and where the Spirit of the Lord is, there is liberty" (emancipation from bondage, freedom) (II Corinthians 3:17 AMP).

When you get the right image of God, it will open heaven up to you, and hell itself will not be able to overcome you when you carry the right image of God in your spirit.

God's government is called the Kingdom of Heaven, which is a place not to be confused with His kingdom and His righteousness, which is a method, or God's way of doing and being right (Matthew 6:33 AMP). When you understand God's character, you will understand and know why God does what He does. You have that ability to know what God is going to do before He does it, because you have the mind of Christ; you have that same anointing on your mind that Jesus has on His mind (John 16:13; I Corinthians 2:16). This is only possible by faith. I John 2:27 says: "But the anointing which ye have received of him abideth in you," and Colossians 2:3 tells us: "In whom [in Christ] are hid all the treasures of wisdom and knowledge." Remember Galatians 2:20 (AMP) where Paul states: "It is not I who lives but Christ (the Messiah) lives in me."

And I John 2:27(AMP) teaches: "But as for you, the anointing (the sacred appointment, the unction) which you received from Him abides [permanently] in you; [so] then you have no need that anyone should instruct you. But just as His anointing teaches you concerning everything and is true and is no falsehood, so you must abide in (live in, never depart from) Him [being rooted in Him, knit to Him], just as [His anointing] has taught you [to do]."

You have that ability in you, because when God created you, He made you in His image and in His likeness (Genesis 1:17). You were created in the likeness and image of God, and He has given you dominion (Genesis 1:16–17; II Corinthians 3:18).

John 4:24 (AMP) tells us that "God is a spirit (a spiritual Being) and those who worship Him must worship Him in spirit and in truth (reality)."

If God is a spirit, and you are made in His likeness, you are also a spirit-being. You live in a body (your earth suit), and you have a soul that consists of your mind, will, and emotions (I Thessalonians 5:23).

And it just keeps getting better, because in II Peter 1:3–11 (AMP), we are given a key so that we might be partakers of the divine nature of God:

> For His divine power has bestowed upon us all things [that are requisite and suited] to life and godliness, through the [full personal] knowledge of Him Who called us by and to His own glory and excellence (virtue).
>
> By means of these He has bestowed on us His precious and exceedingly great promises, so that through them you may escape [by flight] from the moral decay (rottenness and corruption) that is in the world because of covetousness (lust and greed), and become sharers (partakers) of the divine nature.
>
> For this very reason, adding your diligence [to the divine promises], employ every effort in exercising your faith to develop virtue (excellence, resolution, Christian energy), and in [excursing] virtue [develop] knowledge (intelligence).
>
> And in [exercising] knowledge [develop] self-control, and in [exercising] self-control [develop] steadfastness patience, endurance, and [exercising] steadfastness [develop] godliness (piety).
>
> And in [exercising] godliness [develop] brotherly affection and in [exercising] brotherly affection [develop] Christian love.
>
> For as these qualities are yours and increasingly around in you, they will keep [you] from being idle or unfruitful unto the [full personal] knowledge of our Lord Jesus Christ (the Messiah, the Anointed One).
>
> For whoever lacks these qualities is blind, [spiritually] shortsighted, seeing only what is near to him, and has become oblivious [to the fact] that he was cleansed from his old sins.
>
> Because of this, brethren, be all the more solicitous and eager to make sure (to ratify, to strengthen to make steadfast) your calling and election; for if you do this, you will never stumble or fall.
>
> Thus there will be richly and abundantly provided for you entry into the eternal kingdom of our Lord and Savior Jesus Christ.

We are God's future, we are the seed of Abraham, and we are joint heirs with Jesus to the Kingdom of God, His way of doing and being right, and our faith is the measure and condition of our victory in Christ (Romans 8:17). To achieve that great victory, we must have great faith. And that great faith will be ours if we are determined to spend quality time in the Word of God. We must be determined to do all things well and believe in what we are doing. In Mark 7:37, we see that it is recorded that "Jesus has done all things well," and He was able to do this because He believed in what He was doing.

One of the keys that will allow us to do all things well is to encourage ourselves in the Lord on a daily basis. Two records of David encouraging himself in the Lord are found in I Samuel 17:34–37, 45–47; and 30:6–8.

> And David said unto Saul, Thy servant kept his father's sheep, and there came a lion, and a bear, and took a lamb out of the flock:
>
> And I went out after him, and smote him and delivered it out of his mouth: and when he arose against me, I caught him by the beard, and smote him, and slew him.
>
> Thy servant slew both the lion and the bear: and this uncircumcised Philistine shall be as one of them, seeing he hath defied the armies of the living God.
>
> David said moreover, The Lord that delivered me out of the paw of the lion, and out of the paw of the bear, he will deliver me out of the hand of this Philistine.
>
> Then said David to the Philistine, Thou comest to me with a sword, and with a spear, and with a shield: but I come to thee in the name of the Lord of hosts, the God of the armies of Israel, whom thou hast defiled.
>
> This day will the Lord deliver thee into mine hand; and I will smite thee, and take thine head from thee; and I will give the carcasses of the host of the Philistines this day unto the fowls of the air, and to the wild beasts of the earth; and all the earth may know that there is a God in Israel.
>
> And all this assembly shall know that the Lord saveth not with sword and spear: for the battle is the Lord's and he will give you unto our hands.
>
> And David was greatly distressed; for the people spake of stoning him because the soul of all the people was grieved,

every man for his sons and for his daughters: but David encouraged himself in the Lord His God.

And David said to Abiathar the priest, Ahimelech's son, I pray thee, bring me hither the ephod. And Abiathar brought thither the ephod to David.

And David enquired at the Lord, saying, Shall I pursue after this troop? Shall I overtake them? And he answered him, Pursue: for thou shalt surely overtake them, and without fail recover all.

David spoke a positive confession before Saul and Goliath based on his experience. He knew the covenant that he had with God, and he based his confession on that knowledge, which placed a demand on that covenant requiring God to act on his behalf.

Next we see where David's home town, Ziklag, had been destroyed, and his family and the families of his army were carried off by his enemies. I Samual 30:6 tells us that; "David was greatly distressed; for the people spoke of stoning him, because the soul of all the people was grieved, every man for his sons and for his daughters: but David encouraged himself in the Lord his God." How did he do it? He had the priest's son bring him the ephod, which allowed David to go before the Lord and spend quality time inquiring as to what he should do about this situation. As you can see, David followed God's directions and won a great victory.

Under the new covenant that was ratified by Jesus at the cross, we know that:

> ... we have a great high priest, that is passed into the heavens, Jesus the Son of God, let us hold fast our profession.
>
> For we have not a high priest which cannot be touched with the feeling of our infirmities; but was in all points tempted like as we are, yet without sin.
>
> Let us therefore come boldly unto the throne of grace, that we may obtain mercy, and find grace to help in time of need. (Hebrews 4:14–16)

The Amplified Bible states the same passage this way:

> Inasmuch then as we have a great High Priest Who has [already] ascended and passed through the heavens, Jesus the Son of God; let us hold fast our confession [of faith in Him].

For we do not have a High Priest Who is unable to understand and sympathize and have a shared feeling with our weaknesses and infirmities and liability to the assaults of temptation, but One Who has been tempted in every respect as we are, yet without sinning.

Let us then fearlessly and confidently and boldly draw near to the throne of grace (the throne of God's unmerited favor to us sinners), that we may receive mercy [for our failures] and find grace to help in good time for every need [appropriate help and well-timed help, coming just when we need it].

Jesus is your High Priest, and He lives forever to make intercession on your behalf (Hebrews 7:25. There is never a moment when Jesus is not interceding for your success and victory; He is aware of everything that you are facing, and He is making intercession for you right now.

This is how we partake in the divine nature of God. We come boldly to the throne of grace, spending quality time with God and encouraging ourselves in the Lord by speaking words of faith based on what the Word of God tells us.

Verse 16 tells us to "come boldly to the throne of grace." The word *boldly* vividly portrays just how much God wants you to come to Him. *Boldly* comes from the Greek word *parresia* and gives the idea of boldness, frankness, forthrightness, and outspokenness. This clearly means that God wants you to be very direct about telling Him when you need help. And you never have to be timid or fearful about telling the Lord exactly what you are facing and what you need, because He encourages you to speak up and be bold.

Spending quality time with the Lord does not include following after the pleasures of this world doing whatever you feel like doing or going wherever you want to go. It requires you to enter into His presence to worship Him and to make your requests known. It gives you the opportunity to speak freely to God about your problem and how you feel as a result of your situation. Most important is for you to spend quality time listening to what He is telling you. If you want God to move in your life, you need to be doing what He has called you to do.

We are to focus on the solution not the problem. That is how we can make a demand on our covenant just like David did. But much too often, we close ourselves off from the goodness of God, because we fail to encourage ourselves in the Lord on a regular basis. But when we do, we will come to a place in our lives where we are so dependent on the kindness and mercy of God that we will expect it every day.

Every day, in every circumstance, there is a gift from God present in our lives. Often, the more desperate the situation, the greater the gift being offered to us. But, we can easily miss it if we don't apply our faith in looking for it and allowing God to lavish His love upon us (Jeremiah 9:24; Job 23:13; Psalms 139:12).

In Matthew 14:30, we see that Peter began to doubt: "… when he saw the wind boisterous …" He made a mistake by taking his eyes off of Jesus and focusing them on what surrounded him. That is when he felt the strong wind and saw the rough waves. That is when he became fearful. And at the moment Peter became afraid, he began to sink. He quit walking by faith and began walking by sight.

If you will examine your own experiences, you will discover that when you started looking at the symptoms in your body or at your dire situation, you began to waver and doubt God's Word. Walking by sight—paying more attention to the things that you can see, feel, or hear—often causes you to fear. And that fear will cause you to sink. We must be careful not to become resigned to the situations that surround us, but we must constantly look for opportunities to release the power of God that lives in us.

The only way to not be fearful is to keep your eyes on Jesus. You may ask: how can I keep my eyes on Jesus? I can't see Him. God has given us His written Word to unveil the Living Word. "In the beginning was the Word, and the Word was with God, and the Word was God" (John 1:1). You can't know Jesus the way you should without knowing the written Word of God.

Peter took his eyes off of the Word (Jesus) and saw the wind and the waves. Likewise, when you begin to look at the circumstances of life, the symptoms in your body, or at whatever is coming against you, you will also begin to sink.

Miraculously, Peter started to walk on the water, but his doubt stopped the flow of God's power. The supernatural power of God began on Peter's behalf, but Peter failed to continue acting on the Word, so the power of God never reached its full potential in the situation.

God's Word is true: you will have whatever you believe in your heart (Mark 11:22–23). You can believe what God's Word says about your situation, or you can believe what the devil is telling you, which is nothing but doubt and fear. Doubt is actually a belief in itself. The trouble is that it's the wrong belief. Doubt believes that God's Word might not be true—or that God's power might not work for you in your situation. But the good news is that if you can believe the wrong thing, you can also believe he right thing. To make your "believer" work, you have to meditate on God's Word and start believing and confessing the Truth.

God's best for you is for you to receive according to your faith and not by His divine intervention. God's power is always present, and you can receive the miraculous in your life by reaching out with the hand of faith and taking hold of that what belongs to you in Christ Jesus according to God's Word.

We must never allow the world to affect our spirit. Our spirit must take precedent over the situation that we are facing, because "Greater is he that is in me, than he that is in the world" (I John 4:4).

No matter what the situation, God is greater than it is. He lives in us, and our faith in Him will enable us to overcome any situation. We don't have to deny how bad the situation is; we just don't have to be affected by it. We have the right to deny it the right to affect our lives, because God said that He, not the world around us, will supply all our needs according to His riches in glory by Christ Jesus (Philippians 4:19). If the world around you is having a problem, you don't have to join it. He said if we would not doubt in our hearts but believe that those things we say shall come to pass, we shall have then and we will if we don't give up. All that we have to do is to say, "Mountain, be thou removed, be thou cast into the sea" (Mark 11:23). Speak to the mountain by name; call it just what it is, and after we say it, it is up to us to keep any doubt out of our hearts by speaking only those things that God says about the situation. We are simply to believe it and receive it.

Doubt will stop your faith, because it is a chronic condition of the mind, and it acts like a cancerous growth in the spirit that must be cut out with the scalpel of faith. If not, it will cripple you and make you hesitant to do anything.

You must yield yourself to the Spirit and allow spiritual forces to manifest your victory. Be alive unto God and empowered by His might and His Spirit. Take your place and use the Name of Jesus to stand against the forces of evil. "Be strong in the Lord and the power of his might" (Ephesians 6:10).

All of the storms and upheaval, all of the rioting and killings, all of the kidnappings and murders, all of the political chaos, all of the things that are happening on the earth are caused by spiritual forces. And because the church—those who are already alive unto God and empowered by His Spirit—are not taking their places, using the Name of Jesus, and constantly standing against the forces of evil, they are allowing them to move in everywhere they can with the assignment to kill, steal, and destroy (John 10:10).

But if you will stand in the gap and make up the hedge to stand against these things, then they will be turned around. The blessings of God will flow, the Kingdom of God shall be enhanced, and the Church of Jesus Christ shall multiply in numbers and gain momentum. Then men will look and see that the light is shining, the truth of God's Word is going forth, and the Holy Spirit is in manifestation (Luke 1:79).

The key is for us to walk with God daily and be faithful, to learn, and to yield and respond to the leadership of the Holy Ghost. In every area of life, it is impossible to succeed without believing something, and you can't believe anything without words. Words paint pictures and carry authority:

> For by your words you will be justified and acquitted, and by your words you will be condemned and sentenced. (Matthew 12:37 AMP)

> For out of the abundance of the heart the mouth speaketh. (Matthew 12:34)

Your words are the voice of your heart. Your victory will come directly from the Word of God that you have planted in abundance into your heart and the Word of God that you speak out of your mouth. Exercising your faith in God is done by speaking God's Word over any given situation, which is the best way to fight the devil. As you speak the Word of God into God's ear, which is prayer, you are also speaking it right into the face of the devil. When you do that, God will come on the scene and run the devil off.

James 4:7 directs us to "Submit yourselves therefore to God. Resist the devil, and he will flee from you." You submit yourself unto God by spending quality time in the Word and writing it on the tablet of your heart by reading and meditating on the Word. Then when a problem comes up, you quote the Word that is in abundance in your heart to the devil, and he will flee from you as if in terror (Joshua 1:8; Psalms 45:1).

The Word clearly says that we will have troubles in this life. It is how we handle them that will make us victorious. Proverbs 18:21 says: "Death and life are in the power of the tongue." The choice is yours to make. Will you choose life, or will you choose death? Because the power is in your words, you must be cautious and select you words carefully to elevate the answer and not the problem (Deuteronomy 30:19–20).

Words give us something to believe, so don't ever try to separate God from His Word.

Your faith will also grow by hearing God's Word from other people. We played the Bible on tape in our home for several years, twenty-four hours a day, seven days a week. It was played low enough that it wouldn't interfere with our daily activities and conversations but loud enough to build faith in our lives. Teaching tapes can also be used in the same fashion. There is always time during the day—driving to and from work, lunch breaks, etc.—when you have the opportunity to hear the Word preached. But your faith will grow faster when you hear yourself speak the Word of God.

13

THE FULLNESS OF THE BLESSING

Romans 15:29 says: "And I am sure that, when I come unto you, I shall come in the fullness of the blessing of the gospel of Christ."

There are several levels of the blessings of God. "The blessing of the Lord, will make a person rich, and he addeth no sorrow with it" (Proverbs 10:22).

The blessing is an empowerment, and it came on you when you made Jesus the Lord of your life to enable you to do what you could not do in your natural might and achieve what you could not achieve by your own natural ability. The blessing causes you to be different in that it removes the limits placed on you by the unbelieving world. It will allow you to live an extraordinary life as it removes the restrictions of the world. It is designed to take your life to another level and it will enable you to do those things that you cannot do in your own strength. It will open doors for you that no man can shut.

In Romans 15:29, *fullness* means to go to the highest level, without measure, going beyond all previous limits. We have all placed self-induced limitations on our lives. God didn't put them there; His Word says that "all things are possible to him that believeth" (Mark 9:23).

Take the time to make a list of everything that you have ever said that starts with the phrases: I just can't imagine that I will ever have or I could never do that. Compare your list to Psalms 78:41where we are told: "they turned back and tempted God, and limited the Holy One of Israel." Every time you make a statement that limits what God can do in your life, you can be assured that you will never have it or do it. Remember Mark 11:23 where it tells us that if you do not doubt in your heart but believe those things that you say will come to pass, you will have it!

To make the change, you have to make up your mind to talk differently, think differently, and act differently, because: "If thou canst believe, all things are possible to him that believeth" (Mark 9:23).

Ephesians 3:20 tells us: "Now unto Him that is able to do exceeding abundantly above all that we ask or think according to the power that worketh within us." Did you notice that it says "unto Him that is able"? God is able to do things that we can't even begin to imagine, but it begins with the power we gain by believing in him. Jesus told people in His earthly ministry that if they could believe it, they could have it (Mark 9:23 11:23).

Faith is the power that makes it happen. "According to thy faith be it unto you" (Matthew 9:29).

> Now to Him Who, by (in consequence of) the [action of His] power that is at work within us, is able to [carry out His purpose and] do superabundantly, far over and above all that we [dare] ask or think [infinitely beyond our highest prayers, desires, thoughts, hopes, or dreams]. (Ephesians 3:20 AMP)

He can do better than all that you dare dream, your highest ambitions, and your greatest desires. But it is all according to your ability to believe it! If you can't believe it, it won't happen. Stop now and take an inventory of what your words have been telling you? Have they been words that limit you or words that limit what God can do in your life?

How do you get to the place where you can believe that God can take you to the next level, beyond your previous limits, so that the blessing can be on your life without measure? You do it according to the power that works within you! And that power is the faith that is in you—the ability to believe what other people cannot believe.

Matthew 15:28 instructs us to let it: "... be it unto thee even as thou wilt." In other words, if you can conceive it, you can receive it. If you can see it on the inside happening to you, no devil from hell can stop it from happening, and you get to that place by hearing the Word of God over and over again. The more of the Word that you put into your heart, the bigger your faith will become. And the bigger your faith becomes, the bigger you can ask and the bigger that you can dream.

To live in the fullness of the blessing and go beyond all of your previous limits is going to demand that you think bigger, ask bigger, dream bigger, and talk bigger.

And to do this, you must stay focused on what the Holy Spirit is saying to you, you must stay focused on what you are hearing from God, and you must be determined that quitting is not an option. You must be willing to sow toward it.

Everything we do is centered on the law of seed time and harvest. You don't become more spiritual or get closer to God without sowing more time in fellowship with God. You don't develop spiritually without sowing more time in meditation and prayer. You don't get into better health without sowing more time into proper nutrition and exercise. You don't go to the next level financially without sowing more financial seed. One gets to the fullness of the blessing by staying focused and sowing toward it.

THE RIGHTEOUSNESS CONNECTION

Righteousness in its simplest form means that you have believed and accepted into your heart what Jesus did at Calvary—that He was made to be sin that you might be made the righteousness of God. This is not something that you do but is based entirely on what Jesus did (II Corinthians 5:21).

Psalms 34:19 tells us that "Many are the afflictions of the righteous: but the Lord delivereth him out of them all." So when adversity, tests and trials, and challenges come your way, you must have the assurance that the Lord will deliver you out of them all. You must be fully persuaded that what God has promised, He is able also to perform.

Romans 4:20–25 tells us:

> He [Abraham] staggered not at the promise of God through unbelief; but was strong in faith, giving glory to God.
>
> And being fully persuaded that, what he had promised, he was able also to perform.
>
> Therefore it was imputed [attributed] to him for righteousness.
>
> Now it was not written for his sake alone, that it was imputed to him;
>
> But for us also, to whom it shall be imputed [attributed], if we believe on him that raised up Jesus our Lord from the dead;
>
> Who was delivered for our offences, and was raised again for our justification.

Notice in verse 20 that Abraham didn't stagger at the promise of God through unbelief. How did he do that? He did it by giving glory to God.

He delighted himself in the Lord by taking time several times a day to give praise to God and thank Him for what He was doing in his life and for giving him those things that he desired (Psalms 37:4). He understood that thanksgiving is the key to releasing God's supernatural power into his life. He knew to give God the praise before the victory came. He refused to allow doubt and unbelief to be in his life by choosing what he would allow his mind to dwell upon and what words would come out of his mouth (Psalms 22:3, 34:1, 119:164; Philippians 4:8). He did it so much that he became fully persuaded that what God had promised him. He just knew that God would do it!

That is what God expects of us; He expects us to act on the fact that giving Him praise and thanksgiving is the key to releasing His supernatural power into our lives. He expects us to take the time, several times a day, to give Him praise and to thank Him for what He is doing in our lives and for giving us those things that we desire. He expects us to get so saturated with His Word that: "What things soever ye desire, when ye pray, believe that ye receive them, and ye shall have them" (Mark 11:24). He expects us to get so pregnant with the expectation that you just know that "what He has promised, He is able also to perform" (Romans 4:21).

One of the things that He has promised us in Psalms 34:19 is that He would deliver us out of all the afflictions in our lives, because we are the righteous. Notice that He has promised to deliver us out of them all. Not just the big ones or the little ones, but all of them. There are no ifs, ands, or buts attached. He will deliver you out of them all if you will follow Abraham's example. He gives an assurance of this in Matthew 5:6 when He tells us that: "Blessed are they which do hunger and thirst after righteousness for they shall be filled."

We also see in Romans 4:17–22 that Abraham became fully persuaded that God would do what He had promised. The way he became fully persuaded was by calling those things which were not manifest as though they were. And he didn't do it just once!

Verse 17 says, "(As it is written, I have made thee a father of many nations,) before him whom he believed, even God, who quickeneth the dead, and calleth those things which be not as though they were." Here Paul is referring to Genesis 17. You will notice that God called Abram the father of nations before he had the promised child, and He taught Abraham to do the same.

God changed Abram's name to Abraham, which meant "father of nations, or multitude." This was the means He used to convince Abraham to call for what he did not yet have in reality. God had established it by promise, but Abraham had to call it into reality by mixing faith with God's Word.

Every time that he said, "I am Abraham," he was calling things that were not yet manifest. Abraham did not deny that he was old. He didn't go around saying, "I'm not old," because he was old. But he said, "I am Abraham," (father of nations). This was God's method of helping him change his image, and it caused him to be fully persuaded.

Paul also gave us insight into this principle in I Corinthians 1:27–28:

> But God hath chosen the foolish things of the world to confound the wise; and God hath chosen the weak things of the world to confound the things which are mighty;
> And base things of the world, and things which are despised, hath God chosen, yea, and things which are not, to bring to nought things that are.

In other words God uses spiritual forces that are not seen to nullify natural things that are seen. This is the Bible principle of calling things that are not as though they were.

Then in II Corinthians 4:13, Paul says: "We have the same spirit of faith, according as it is written, I believe, and therefore have I spoken; we also believe, and therefore speak." Paul is quoting David when he said, "I believed, and therefore have I spoken." In Psalms 118:17, David also said, "I shall not die, but live, and declare the works of the Lord."

When it comes to divine healing, this is a vital principle. We should declare to ourselves what God's Word reveals about us, regardless of the circumstances or how we feel about it.

In Romans 10:6–8, Paul says that the righteousness that is of faith says "the word is nigh thee, even in thy mouth and in thy heart." Notice that the Word is first in your mouth and then in your heart. God's Word becomes engrafted into your heart as you speak it. When you speak it, you also hear it, and there is nothing more important to your faith than declaring what God has said about you with your own voice. Giving voice to God's Word is a method of calling for things that God has given us by promise but have not yet been manifest.

When you do this, some would say that you are denying what exists, but that's not true at all. You are establishing what God has said to be true concerning healing or whatever, even though it is not yet a reality in your body. You don't deny that sickness exists, but you deny its right to exist in your body, because you have been redeemed from the curse of the law and delivered from the authority of darkness (Galatians 3:13; Colossians 1:13).

God has also given you all things that pertain to life and godliness. These things belong to you (II Peter 1:3–4). When you are sick and confess that you are healed by the stripes of Jesus, you are calling for what God has already given you, even though it is not yet manifest (I Peter 2:24).

This is God's method of calling things that are not as though they were until they are. But there are those that do not understand this principle, and they call things that are the way they are. In short, they deny what exists, and by doing this, they are establishing the present condition or circumstance in their hearts, minds, and bodies. But there is no power in denying that sickness or lack exists. The power is in calling for your need to be met or for healing and health by mixing faith with God's Word.

If you are sick, you don't deny that you are sick; yet, on the other hand, you don't want to always be confessing your sickness, for that will establish your present circumstance to you. Denying sickness won't make you well. But by mixing faith with God's Word, you are calling for the promise of God to be manifest in your body. This will cause you to be fully persuaded, and healing will be the result.

There are some who don't know any better who say that you are lying if you confess that you are healed when you are sick. But in reality, you are simply calling for the healing that God has already provided for you, even though it is not yet manifest in your body. What you are really doing is practicing God's medicine or doing things God's way.

You are not trying to convince anyone that you are not sick, but you are simply proclaiming what God has said in His Word to be a fact, regardless of your present condition. The Word says, "… by whose (Jesus') stripes ye *were* healed" (Isaiah 53:5; Matthew 8:17; I Peter 2:24). Did you notice that it is in the past tense as far as God is concerned but not yet manifest in your body.

You are just calling your body healed and well according to Luke 17:5–6 and Mark 11:23. Your body is listening to you, and it will obey you if you will believe and not doubt in your heart. Your words will always have more effect on your body than anyone else's words.

Your body was created with the ability to heal itself, and if every part functions properly, it will. Some sickness is caused by a chemical imbalance in the body, and the part of the brain that controls the speech also controls the secretion of chemicals to the body. This sheds some more light on what Jesus said in Mark 11:23: "… he shall have whatsoever he saith."

Confess: My immune system and every organ of my body work to the perfection that God created them to work and my body is in perfect chemical balance.

THE FULLNESS OF THE BLESSING IS YOURS WHEN YOU SPEAK THE DESIRED EFFECTS

One of the biggest mistakes that most Christians make is to call things that are the way they are, and by doing that, they are establishing the present condition or circumstance in their hearts, minds, and bodies. It is simply a fact that they are giving instructions to their bodies and their immune systems that will eventually respond to those instructions.

Jesus said, "I have told my people they can have what they say," (Mark 11:23) but My people are saying what they have. The Word of God conceived in the human spirit, formed by the tongue, and spoken out of the mouth becomes creative power that will work for you every time.

The enemy occasionally only has to plant a thought on one's mind to get them to start confessing that there is something wrong with them.

There is more truth to Mark 11:23 than most people realize. You can have what you say in faith, but most people are just saying what they have. God created the universe by this method. God released His faith in words. You and I are created in the image of God; therefore, we release our faith in words. Our words are the most powerful things in the universe today.

John 16:33 (AMP) says, "I have told you these things, so that in Me you may have [perfect] peace and confidence. In the world you have tribulation and trials and distress and frustration; but be of good cheer [take courage; and be confident, certain, undaunted]! For I have overcome the world. [I have deprived it of power to harm you and have conquered it for you." As you read and meditate on this verse, you should recognize that tests are going to come your way, but defeat and failure are not in your future.

You should never deny that trouble, tribulation, affliction, tragedy, or even challenges will come into your life. But you can deny their right to bring defeat into your life and rob you of your victory in Christ after what Jesus has done for us at Calvary.

I Peter 4:12 (AMP) says: "Beloved, do not be amazed and bewildered at the fiery ordeal which is taking place to test your quality, as though something strange (unusual and alien to you and our position) were befalling you."

When these tests and trials, these adversities and challenges, come, don't think it strange, because it is all part of being a Christian in this world. You are going to be faced with adversity.

II Corinthians 4:8–9 tells us that:

We are troubled on every side, yet not distressed; we are perplexed, but not in despair.

Persecuted, but not forsaken; cast down, but not destroyed.

Notice that both Jesus and Paul agree that we will have challenges and we will face adversities, but we have been instructed to "Be of good cheer [take courage; and be confident, certain, undaunted]! For I have overcome the world. [I have deprived it of power to harm you and have conquered it for you.]" (John 16:33 AMP).

To be of good cheer is going to require you to look beyond the circumstances, because it is not part of our human nature to look beyond our circumstances and have peace and joy and be of good cheer. One must train himself by reading and meditating God's Word to look beyond the problems in his life and keep his attention on what God has promised.

We are instructed to walk by faith, not by sight (II Corinthians 5:7). That means that we have the ability to look beyond those circumstances and know by the authority of God's Word that there is something on the other side of them that can't be seen in the natural. And that something is victory in Christ!

You have to keep your eyes on the promises of God and not on the circumstances, or you will never see the victory that is on the other side.

In Mark 4:35–41, we see where Jesus and the disciples were on the sea when a great storm arose:

> And the same day, when the even was come, he said unto them, Let us pass over unto the other side.
>
> And when they had sent away the multitude, they took him even as he was in the ship. And there were also with him other little ships.
>
> And there arose a great storm of wind, and the waves beat into the ship, so that it was now full.
>
> And he was in the hinder part of the ship, asleep on a pillow; and they awake him, and say unto him, Master carest thou not that we perish?
>
> And he arose, and rebuked the wind, and said unto the sea, Peace, be still. And the wind ceased, and there was a great calm.
>
> And he said unto them, why are ye so fearful? How is it that ye have no faith?

> And they feared exceedingly, and said one to another, what manner of man is this, that even the wind and the sea obey him?

Notice that Jesus and the disciples were in this boat when a great storm arose and frightened the disciples to such a point that they woke Jesus up and asked Him if He cared about their safety. I believe that they thought that the ship was going down with them in it.

Jesus got up and rebuked the wind and told the sea to be still. The wind ceased, and there was a great calm. Then He asked the disciples where their faith was.

In verse 37, it says that there was a great storm. In the Greek, the word *great* means mega. After Jesus spoke to the storm, there came a "great calm." The word *great* here has the same meaning, mega, which leads us to believe that on the other side of every great storm, there is a great calm. After every great attack, there is a great victory. Great victories are always preceded by great attacks! This is where we need to know how to put on our armor and charge the enemy.

In I Samuel 17:41–48, we see where David told Goliath that he would take his head from him and give the carcasses to the fowls of the air and to the wild beasts of the earth. He did that so they would know that there was a God in Israel. David then said that the battle was the Lord's, and he ran toward the army of the Philistines and to a great victory.

You will only get your victory when you run toward your enemies and declare that the battle is the Lord's and the victory is yours. You have a mighty helper called the Holy Ghost in you and you swing that twoedged sword against the enemy when you speak the Word of God and make a positive confession of faith based on that Word.

Don't just stand by and allow the enemies of God to gain control over you or allow the demons from hell to defy the promises of God when all that you have to do is stand up and say, "Wait a minute, devils. I have had enough of sickness; I have had enough of disease; I have had enough of poverty. This day, bless God, the battle is the lord's, and the victory is mine."

In Matthew 16:19 (AMP), Jesus said: "I will give unto thee the keys of the kingdom of Heaven; and whatever you bind (declare to be improper and unlawful) on earth must be what is already bound in heaven; and whatever you loose (declare lawful) on earth must be what is already loosed in heaven." Remember from earlier, A key, from the Greek word *kleis*, "a key" is used to mean; knowledge of the revealed will of God, by which men enter into the life that pleases God. Those keys represent your God-given power here on this earth. Keys are a symbol of authority, and God has given you the power to both bind and loose things here on this earth.

Jesus gave you the authority to use His name. Therefore, in the name of the Lord Jesus Christ, you have the authority to bind the principalities, powers, and rulers of the darkness of this world. You have the authority to cast down spiritual wickedness in high places and render it harmless and ineffective against you in the name of Jesus and you do that by using right words (Matthew 16:19; John 16:23–24; Ephesians 6:12).

You activate that power by choosing words that line up with the Word of God, and you run toward your giant while believing God, telling the enemy just who you are in Christ and speaking out those promises that God has made to you. If you don't, fear will creep up and destroy you. But if you keep coming at the devil, he is going to fall by your side where you can cut his head off and show those around you how they can get ahead in life.

But you have to run toward your giant dressed in the armor that God has provided for you. You can't run away from him. Never back up; instead, keep going forward, believing that God's Word will not return to Him void. No matter what! (Isaiah 55:11).

When we fight for God, He will fight for us. When we fight by God's rules, we can take it to the bank that Jesus Christ is going to fight for us and ensure our victory, because we are seated at the right hand of the Father with Jesus. When He hears those words of faith, He is obligated to cause them to come to pass in our lives.

Cast your cares upon the Lord, because He cares for you. Tell the Lord about your problems and why He is obligated to do something about them based on His Word. He already knows it, but it is for your benefit that you tell Him (Psalms 55:22, 118:5; I Peter 5:7).

We must run head on at the problems in our lives teamed up with Jesus and solve them instead of just standing on the sidelines watching them go by.

Talk to the problems—those mountains in your life—and tell them that you are coming against them in the Name of the Lord God Jehovah, and the victory is yours. Because if you don't live like you have the victory in Christ, you will never see it. Just talking to the problem once in a while or every now and then will seldom lead you to victory. You have to be determined to get in and stay in the fight until you win

It is possible to be unarmed in the estimation of men while we fight for God, because we can confidently expect that He will fight for us. And when we fight for God, we can take it to the bank that Jesus Christ is going to fight for us. But the world will tell us that we cannot win this battle, because they do not know and understand God's will for us (Deuteronomy 10:12–13; III John 1:2).

They don't know about III John 1:2, which says: "Beloved, I wish above all things that you may prosper and be in health, as thy soul prospers." They don't know that God uses spiritual forces that are not seen to nullify natural things that are seen. This is the Bible principle of calling things that are not as though they were (Romans 4:17).

They don't know that we have God's armor and weapons at our disposal. Armor and weapons that are both offensive and defensive in nature. These pieces of armor and weapons are listed here one by one with an explanation of just what each piece represents.

Ephesians 6:10–18 also instructs us in the assembling, maintenance and use of these weapons.

Verse 10 directs us to:

> Finally, my brethren, be strong in the Lord, and in the Power
> of His might.

Finally here means this is final; we must do it now. In conclusion, I have saved the most important issue of this epistle until the end of the letter, so if you remember nothing else that I have said, you will remember this. I want this to stand out in your mind.

Could you use some extra strength today? *Strong* is from the Greek *endunamao,* which is a compound of the words *en* and *dunamis.* The word *en* means in, and the word *dunamis* means explosive strength, ability, and power. It's where we get the word *dynamite.*

This word *endunamao* shows us a picture of an explosive power that is being deposited into some type of container, vessel, or other form of receptacle. The nature of this word means that there must be some type of receiver for this power.

Now this is where we come into the picture! We were specially fashioned and designed by God to be the receptacles of that divine power. This is what makes man different from the animals. God formed man of the dust of the ground and breathed into his nostrils, and man became a living soul (Genesis 2:7), a container especially fashioned and designed to possess that explosive, Holy Spirit power.

To be strong in the Lord is to receive a supernatural, strengthening, internal deposit of power into your inner man. God is the giver of this power, and we are the receptacles into which this power is to be deposited, and it ours for the asking!

When Paul wrote this verse, he knew that we would desperately need this supernatural power in order to successfully combat all of the attacks of the enemy. That is why he urges us to open up our spirits. God's desire is to restore us to favor with Him, so we can act as His ambassadors on earth. As such, this is how we need to look at ourselves: as emissaries from a foreign land. I Peter 2:11 (AMP) calls us "aliens and strangers here," because this earth is not our home. We are merely passing through and as such we are to present our souls and our bodies to God so that we can receive His supernatural strength. In II Corinthians 12:8, God told Paul: "My grace is sufficient for thee: for my strength is made perfect in weakness."

> Verse 11: Put on the whole armour of God, that ye may be able to stand against the wiles of the devil.

Here we are directed to put on the whole armor of God. The phrase *whole armor* is from the Greek *panaplia*, and it refers to a Roman soldier who is fully dressed in his armor from head to toe. It is the word *pan,* which means all, combined with the word *hoplos,* which is Greek for armor. Together they form the word *panoplia,* which is recognized as the word to describe the full attire and weaponry of a Roman soldier, although it does not describe all of the weapons that were at his disposal.

Likewise, we have been given the whole armor of God, essentially everything that we would ever need to successfully combat the opposing forces of the enemy. As we continue with the lesson, note that every piece of armor has great significance for us in our battle, and it is our responsibility to put the armor on and always keep it clean and in good repair for immediate use.

Take a minute and think about what the devil must think when he sees you coming at him dressed in the full armor of God: your face shield down, swinging the double-edged sword, with the Word of God coming out of your mouth. Does he really have any choice but to believe that Jesus is after him again? Remember: "you are in Him, made full and having come to fullness of life [in Christ you too are filled with the Godhead—Father, Son and Holy Spirit—and reach full spiritual stature]. And He is the Head of all rule and authority [of every angelic principality and power]" (Colossians 2:10 AMP).

> Verse 12: For we wrestle not against flesh and blood, but against principalities, against powers, against the rulers of the darkness of this world, against spiritual wickedness in high places.

Spiritual warfare is real! The devil and his demon spirits are real. They are real beings that hate the human race, because man was created in the likeness and image of God (Genesis 1:26). They roam about seeking whom they might destroy. That is why is so important for you to know how to use the armor and the weapons that God has provided for you to protect yourself against their attacks.

Most of those attacks will occur in your mind, because the devil is a flesh devil and not a spirit devil. He knows that your mind is the central control center for your life; therefore, if he can take control of one small area of your mind, he can expand outward into other weak areas that have not been strengthened by the Holy Spirit and the Word of God.

By poisoning your mind with doubt and unbelief, he will be able to create strongholds from which he will be able to manipulate not only your mind, but also your emotions and your body. Understand that your mind is the strategic center where the battle of spiritual warfare is won or lost!

We wrestle not against flesh and blood. The word *wrestle* is from the Greek word *pale*, which refers to struggling, wrestling, or hand-to-hand combat. And the word *pate* is also the word from which the Greeks delivered their name for the *Palasra*, which was a huge palace of combat sports that was situated in the center of larger ancient cities.

Almost all of the sporting events that were held in these places were fought to the death. There were few if any rules, and it was expected of the loser not only to lose the match but his life also. Thus, we must understand that spiritual warfare can be a bitter struggle and an intense conflict.

Principalities, powers, rulers of the darkness, and spiritual wickedness in high places are the four forces of darkness that work covertly behind most disasters and many moral failures.

Principalities, taken from the Greek *archai,* is used to depict individuals who hold the highest and loftiest positions of rank and authority. These evil spirits are at the very top of Satan's kingdom, and they are powerful evil beings that have probably held their lofty positions since the fall of Satan.

Powers, from the Greek *exousia*, means delegated authority. This describes a lower, second-level group of evil beings or demon spirits, who have received this delegated authority from Satan to carry out all manner of evil in whatever way they so desire.

The rulers of the darkness of this world describes the rank and file of Satan's followers and depicts raw power that has been harnessed and put into some kind of order. It gives the picture of raw manpower being converted into an organized, disciplined army—one that is being trained to do damage to the human race.

Spiritual wickedness in high places—*wickedness* is taken from the word *poneros* and is used to depict something that is bad, vile, malevolent, vicious, impious, and malignant. This gives us insight to the ultimate aim of Satan's dark domain. These evil spirits are sent forth to afflict us with their bad, vile, malevolent, vicious, impious, and malignant ways.

In John 10:10, we can see just what Jesus meant when He said that: "The thief cometh not, but for to steal, and to kill, and to destroy." What is more important to understand is that Jesus came "that we might have life, and that we might have it more abundantly" (James 1:17).

What we, the Church of Jesus Christ, lack is order and discipline. Jesus has given us power and authority over all of the demonic spirits and their powers (Luke 10:19). We have that same power that raised Jesus from the dead living in us (Romans 8:5), but very few Christians are prepared to do the enemy any serious damage. To do so, we must discipline ourselves and be prepared to listen to the voice of God's Spirit; we must be prepared to gird up the loins of our minds and fill our thoughts with the Word of God and be determined to see ourselves as soldiers in the army of God. And when you are ready to witness the awesome demonstration of God's power in your life, you will prevail against Satan's rank and file.

The victory is yours, because these demonic spirits cannot do anything unless you allow your flesh to cooperate with them! They may come in to tempt you, to seduce you, to deceive you, and to assault your mind, but unless they find a partner willing to listen to or cooperate with them, their evil attempts are futile and powerless.

The key that I have found that works all of the time when the devil wages the battle against me is to keep my mind dominated by the Word of God. I speak the Word out loud so that my mind has to stop and listen to what my mouth is saying. This blocks the devil's ability to plant thoughts into my mind. In Joshua 1:8, we are told to mediate the Word of God day and night or to keep our mind dominated by the Word of God. As you do that, your flesh will be kept under the control of the Holy Spirit, which will block the enemy's attacks against your mind.

This is what is meant in I Peter 1:13 where we are encouraged to "gird up the loins of your mind." You control what your mind thinks about by spending quality time in the Word of God, reading and meditating the Word until it is planted firmly in your spirit, and then when you hear the devil coming against you, you resist him by simply quoting that Word to him, and he will flee from you.

You can easily check up on yourself by just paying attention to the first thing that comes into your mind and out of your mouth when something unexpected happens. Was it a positive thought in line with the Word of God, or was it something negative planted there by the enemy?

> Verse 13: Wherefore take unto you the whole armour of God, that ye may be able to withstand in the evil day, and having done all, to stand.

We are instructed here to "take unto you the whole armour of God." A half-dressed soldier is not so nearly effective in battle as one that has all of his armor and weapons available to protect himself and do battle with the enemy. An army's most effective weapon is to search out and take advantage of the enemy's weak points, because they know that those weak points are where the enemy is most vulnerable and most susceptible to attack or damage.

As such, the devil is always scouting out your weak points, looking for a successful way of attacking you. But when you take unto you the whole armor of God, there is nothing for the enemy to find, because you are totally protected!

We are to stand ready to do battle with the enemy at a moment's notice. We are not to allow ourselves to get sloppy or lazy. We are to be constantly cleaning and maintaining our armor and equipment. In other words, we are to stay in the Word of God, reading it, hearing it, and meditating on it and keeping ourselves in constant fellowship with God.

God knows that we will mess up, and He has made provisions for us to get back into fellowship with Him. We only need to confess that we missed it, repent of our wrongdoing, and return to our place of sonship with the Father (I John 1:9).

> Verse 14: Stand therefore, having your loins girt about with truth, and having on the breastplate of righteousness:

As you study the Word of God, you will discover that having your loins girt about with truth, God's Word, is the most vital piece of weaponry that you can possess. The loin belt was designed to hold many of the other pieces of your weaponry together, and without it, your spiritual armor would literally come apart piece by piece. Knowing that your loin belt is securely fastened gives you the assurance that all of the other pieces of equipment will stay in place, enabling you to move quickly and fight the enemy with great fury.

As you go into battle for the Lord, you will understand why it is so important that you understand that He requires you to have your loins girt about with truth, which is the written Word of God. You must allow God's Word to have a central place in your life, where it will give you a sense of righteousness that will cover you like a mighty breastplate. When the Word of God is operating in your life, it will give you the sword that you need, that *rhema* word which will be quickened to your heart by the Holy Spirit.

If you will allow God's Word to dominate your thinking, it will give you a peace, a piece that passeth all understanding, that will protect your heart and mind from the attacks of the enemy (Philippians 4:7).

As long as the loin belt of truth, The Word of God is central in your life, the rest of your spiritual armor will be effective. But the day that you begin to ignore God's Word and stop applying it to your life, you will start to lose your sense of righteousness and peace, and you will find the devil attacking your mind on a regular basis, filling it with lies and vain imaginations.

It is your responsibility to keep the Word of God in its rightful place at the very core of your life, and if you don't, you will soon find your armor literally coming apart at the seams. There is nothing more important than spending quality time in the Word of God every day!

> Verse 15: And your feet shod with the preparation of the gospel of peace;

The word *shod* is derived from the word *hupodeomai*, a compound of the words *hupo* and *deo*. The word *hupo* means under, and *deo* means to bind. Taken together as one word, it conveys the idea of binding something very tightly on the bottom of one's feet. Therefore, this is not the picture of a loosely fitting shoe but of a shoe that has been tied onto the bottom of the foot extremely tightly.

The word *preparation* is the Greek *etoimasin,* and it presents the idea of readiness or preparation. It portrays men of war who have their shoes tied on very tightly to ensure a firm footing. Once you have the assurance that your shoes are going to stay in place, you are ready to march out onto the battlefield and confront to enemy.

You prepare yourself by meditating on those verses pertaining to who and what you are in Christ. And by doing so you are preparing yourself to fight the good fight of faith knowing that God is backing you to the hilt.

> Verse 16: Above all, taking the shield of faith, wherewith ye shall be able to quench all the fiery darts of the wicked.

The word *shield* is the Greek word *thureos,* which was used by the Greeks and Romans to depict an oblong door that was both wide and long. It was big enough to cover the man carrying it to protect him from the weapons of his enemy. As such, God has given us a shield of enough faith to make certain that we are completely covered for every situation. We are able to quench all the fiery darts of the wicked.

In Romans 12:3, Paul tells us that "God hath dealt to every man the measure of faith." He has given us enough faith to make sure that we are covered for any event that comes along in life! But it is our responsibility to maintain it and care for it and keep it in good shape so that it is available to use at a moment's notice. To do this requires us to daily apply a fresh coat of the anointing of the Holy Spirit, for without a fresh touch of God's Spirit upon our lives, our faith will become hard, stiff, and brittle and will be worthless to us.

We know that our faith comes by hearing the Word of God on a regular basis, and it is our individual responsibility to take the time on a daily basis to read and meditate on the Word to receive a fresh anointing, or a fresh protective covering of our faith.

Notice that, "…wherewith ye shall be able to quench all the fiery darts of the wicked." The first part of this Greek phrase *wherewith* would be better translated "by which." For the words "ye shall be able," the Greek word used here is the word *dunamis*, which denotes explosive power or dynamic power and is where we get the word "dynamite." Ephesians 6:16 could actually be translated: Above all, taking the shield of faith, by which you will be dynamically empowered. When you lift your shield of faith high and hold it out in front of you where it belongs, it will divinely energize you to stand bravely against every assault of the devil. That shield of faith will become dynamically and supernaturally empowered to act as in impenetrable wall of defense against the enemy's tactics.

That shield of faith is so powerful that it makes you fortified, invulnerable, and armed to the teeth. It equips you to hold a solid position. It turns you into a spiritual fortress so that you have the ability to move your position forward without being hit by any of the enemy's missiles.

It doesn't mean that the devil won't try to stop you, but when the shield of faith is held out in front of you as it was designed to be, you will become divinely empowered to "quench all the fiery darts of the wicked."

The word *quench* is from the Greek *shennume*, which means to quench by dousing or to extinguish by drowning in water. It refers to the water-soaked shield of the Roman soldiers, as just before they went into battle they soaked their shields in water until they were completely saturated. A wet shield has the ability to douse the fiery flames of the enemy.

Romans 10:17 says that our faith comes and is increased by hearing the Word of God, and in Ephesians 5:26, the Word of God is likened to water. So as we regularly submit ourselves to the Word of God, we soak our faith with the Word just as the soldiers did. And when our faith becomes waterlogged or Word-saturated, it becomes fire resistant to every fiery dart that will be thrown against us.

The words *fiery darts* are from the Greek *belos*, which refers to an arrow with its tip wrapped with fabric soaked in flammable fluids so it will burn with hot and angry flames.

You can refuse to let yourself become the devil's victim. You just need to hold your Word-doused shield of faith high in front of you so it completely covers your life. Then you can rest assured that no fiery darts of the devil will make any serious impact on you, because through the dynamic, explosive power of God, your faith shield will protect you from anything that the enemy throws at you!

> Verse 17: And take the helmet of salvation, and the sword of
> the Spirit, which is the Word of God;

In this verse we are instructed to "take the helmet of salvation," which is a supernatural protection wrapped so tightly around your head that it would safeguard your mind from every mental assault of the enemy. And your salvation is the most gorgeous, most intricate, most elaborate, most ornate gift that God has ever given to you, and it is designed to protect your head. But if you don't walk in all that your salvation entails, you will soon feel the brunt of the enemy's weapon as it comes to attack your mind and steal your victory.

This verse also requires you to take "the sword of the Spirit, which is the Word of God." The word *sword* is the Greek word *machaira*, which is a weapon of murder that caused the victim horrid pain and death. By using the word *machaira* in Ephesians 6:17, Paul is telling us that God has given us, the Church of Jesus Christ, a weapon that is extremely frightful to the devil and his forces. This weapon is so horrific to the kingdom of darkness because it has the razor-sharp power to slash the demonic foes to shreds. The word *machaira* denotes a sword that was dagger-shaped and normally employed in close combat.

The sword of the Spirit is the Word of God. The term *word* is from the Greek *rhema*, which describes something that is spoken clearly and vividly, in unmistakable terms and in undeniable language. In the New Testament, the word *rhema* carries the idea of a quickened word.

Ephesians 6:17 conveys the impression that the Holy Spirit will place a short twoedged razor-sharp sword at your disposal anytime the enemy gets too close and this sword's power will be available the moment the Spirit quickens a specific word for the specific situation that you are facing (Hebrews 4:12).

Verse 18: Praying always with all prayer and supplication in the spirit, and watching thereunto with all perseverance and supplication for all saints.

The word *prayer* is a translation of the word *proseuche*, which is a compound of the words *pros* and *euche*. The word *pros* is a preposition that means toward and can denote a sense of closeness, such as the relationship that exists between the Godhead.

The word *pros* as used here gives us a picture of our close contact with the unseen, demonic spirits that have been drawn up against us referred to in Ephesians 6:12. You will find that almost everywhere in the New Testament where the word *pros* is used it carries the meaning of close, up-front, intimate contact with someone else.

The word *euche* describes a wish, desire, prayer, or vow. Prayer is how we come face to face into close contact with God. It is a vehicle to bring us to a place whereby we may enjoy a close, intimate relationship with God where one yields himself entirely to God. Prayer is more than a simple prayer request. It requires us to surrender, to be willing to change, to consecrate ourselves to and give thanks to God up front for who He is and what He is doing for us before we ever see the answer.

The idea of the word *proseuche* is to come face to face with God and surrender your life in exchange for His. Maintain an attitude of consecration as an ongoing part of your life and be sure to give Him all of the praise and thanks in advance for moving in and on your life.

The Amplified Bible starts out verse 18 this way: "Pray at all times (on every occasion, in every season) in the spirit, with all [manner of] prayer and entreaty." Praying always, with all prayer and supplication is using prayer effectively. It is using the Word of God as if it were a lance being thrown into the spirit realm against the malicious or spiteful works of the adversary. By forcibly hurling this divine instrument of prayer into the face of the enemy, a believer can exert great spiritual power, literally attacking the devil from a distance in order to stop major obstacles from developing up close in his personal life.

There are several forms of prayer available to the believer to use in the good fight of faith (I Timothy 6:12). There is the prayer of faith, the prayer of agreement, the prayer of intercession, the prayer of supplication, the prayer of petition, the prayer of consecration, the prayer of thanksgiving, united prayer, and praying in the Spirit. And we are to use every form of prayer that has been made available to us as it is needed. No one prayer is better than the others, as each one serves a different and necessary purpose in the life of faith.

I encourage you to study the purpose and use of each type of prayer and apply them to your life in Christ, because prayer is a vital piece of your spiritual weaponry. If you should neglect this strategic piece of weaponry, you will find that the enemy will keep attacking you from up close. As you learn to pray and develop a relationship with the Holy Spirit, listening for Him to show you things to come (John 16:13), you will develop an ability to strike the enemy from a distance and therefore maintain a victorious position in your life.

God has placed the weapon of prayer at your disposal so that you can be assured of absolute victory. As you use your weapons of prayer and supplication (Philippians 4:6) in all of their various forms, you will continually reinforce Jesus Christ's triumphant victory over Satan and gloriously demonstrate Satan's miserable defeat in every area of your life.

Jesus defeated the devil, and when you are wearing the armor of God, the devil just doesn't know who is in there. If you were the devil and came across someone wearing the armor of God, with God's helmet on and pulled down, wielding God's weapons in his hands, speaking God's Words, wouldn't you think that God was there?

You must know your enemy and always be on the attack. Never set yourself up in a defensive position but always attack and keep your enemy confused and on the defensive. Notice that God's armor only protects your front side and is designed for you to always being on the attack.

God has given you the ability to be more than a conqueror. II Corinthians 9:8 (AMP) explains that "God is able to make all grace (every favor and earthly blessing) come to you in abundance, so that you may always and under all circumstances and whatever the need to be self-sufficient [possessing enough to require no aid or support and furnished in abundance for every good work and charitable donation]."

The power of God is invincible, and the gifts of the Spirit have been given to us, the Church, as the weapons of our warfare. However, the Church today is going into battle without a true knowledge of God's grace or the training to use those weapons that are available to them. Any time you go to battle without your weapons properly functioning, you cannot expect to win the fight.

The ministry Jesus performed on this earth was directed, guided, and energized by the Holy Spirit—the same Holy Spirit that we have in us today. We can expect to do the same works that Jesus did if we will follow the example that He left for us.

We have a right to every gift of the Holy Spirit, without exception. That is our right in Christ. We are to clothe ourselves in the gifts of the Spirit and go out against the enemy and destroy him. In Zechariah 4:6 (AMP), we are told: "It is not by might [or organization], nor by power [or a decision of a board], but by my spirit, saith the Lord of hosts."

Remember, on the other side, there is a great victory, and you must be able to look past the circumstances to be able to see that victory through the eye of your faith. Paul said in II Corinthians 4:8–9 that we are troubled on every side, yet not distressed; we are perplexed, sometimes we just do not know what to do, but we are not in despair. We are persecuted but nor forsaken. Sometimes we are cast down but not destroyed, knocked down but never knocked out. We will often experience trying times, but God has a solution to all of that. He never leaves us helpless, and He doesn't leave us hopeless.

Nobody is ever going to be entirely free from adversity, challenges, or attacks from the enemy. Notice again in Psalms 34:19 that we are told: "Many are the afflictions of the righteous: but the Lord delivereth him out of them all." When we stand on God's Word and do not give up in the face of problems, God will always deliver us out of them.

Read John 16:33 (AMP) again: "In the world you have tribulation and trials and distress and frustration; but be of good cheer [take courage; and be confident, certain, undaunted]! For I have overcome the world. [I have deprived it of power to harm you and have conquered it for you."

Remember: defeat is not in your future. Trouble will come, but it has no right to rob you of victory or bring defeat into your life. Not after what Jesus said—take courage, be certain, be confident, be undaunted, don't be subdued by fear, and remain competent and courageous. Why? Because Jesus has already deprived those tests, trials, challenges, adversities, and tribulations of their right to harm you.

It's your choice to either believe and act on what Jesus has said or believe something else and do nothing. God has a solution for any problem in your life, and He has provided you with everything that you need to overcome these situations and go past them coming out on the other side in victory. Those that fail either don't know these principles or are simply not acting on them. It is bad not to know these principles, but it is even worse to not act on them.

We should get up in the morning and the darkness surrounding us should come to attention as we call upon the wisdom and power of God to carry us through the day in victory. But to accomplish this we must switch our thinking from "what do I have to defend myself from today?" to living each day focused in faith on God and His plans for my life. We accomplish this by praising Him for His goodness and yielding ourselves to the guidance and leadership of the Holy Spirit throughout the day.

The key is to not magnify the problem or focus on the tribulation but focus on the fact that Jesus has overcome the world for you (John 16:33). Don't deny that the problem exists, because it is real, but refuse to talk about it all of the time and instead talk to that mountain in your life and rejoice in what God is doing. Don't spend your time thinking and talking about your problems but think and talk about what Jesus has said and done for you. Look past the challenge and see the victory. "While we look not at the things which are seen, but at the things which are not seen: for the things which are seen are temporal [subject to change, brief and fleeting, not permanent]; but the things which are not seen are eternal" (II Corinthians 4:18). We are to: "Walk by faith and not by sight" (II Corinthians 5:7).

Challenges should be welcomed into your life to strengthen you to show that you can be victorious in every area of life. That problem you are going through is not permanent; it's temporal and it is subject to change, and it will not last forever. But the Word of God is forever; Jesus Christ is the same yesterday, today, and forever. And if you will faithfully apply the Word of God and your faith to that problem, it will be gone before you know it! (Hebrews 13:8; John 1:14; I John 5:7).

14

PRAYING FOR OTHERS

To pray without exercising your faith is wasting your time. You must believe that God will do what you are asking Him to do, because when you act in faith, God reacts because your faith puts a demand on God's power!

I Timothy 2:1–4 (AMP) tells us:

> First of all, then, I admonish and urge that petitions, prayers, intercessions, and thanksgivings be offered on behalf of all men.
>
> For kings and all who are in positions of authority or high responsibility, that [outwardly] we may pass a quiet and undisturbed life [and inwardly] a peaceable one in all godliness and reverence and seriousness in every way.
>
> For such [praying] is good and right, and [it is] pleasing and acceptable to God our Savior.
>
> Who wishes all men to be saved and [increasingly] to perceive and recognize and discern and know precisely and correctly the [divine] Truth [the Word of God].

As a born-again son of God, you are alive unto God and have been empowered by His Spirit to take your place and use the name of Jesus to stand against the forces of evil to prevent them from moving in and taking over.

As you stand in the gap and take up the hedge of protection over those you are praying for, the conditions that you are seeing will be turned around, and the blessings of God will flow into these people's lives. You will also see the Kingdom of God enhanced, and the Church of Our Lord Jesus Christ multiplied in number and gain momentum. And as you do this, men will see your light shine as the truth of God's Word goes forth in great power with the Holy Ghost in manifestation.

There are many people out there who have chosen not to follow Jesus Christ and make Him their Lord and Savior—many because they have never heard the Gospel preached, some who have allowed Satan (the god of this world) to blind their minds so that they cannot see "the light of the gospel of the glory of Christ," and many who have simply decided to make Satan their spiritual leader (II Corinthians 4:3–4).

Everybody either serves God or Satan; if you don't choose to make the decision, it will be made for you. The satanic side of spiritual warfare is carried out by people Satan controls. He cannot do it by himself. He must find people he can possess to accomplish his evil works through.

You cannot interfere with another person's will, but you can play hell with those demon spirits that are influencing his life. There is no prayer that you can pray that will change the will of another human being, although a prayer of intercession can interfere with the demonic forces that are influencing him.

You can also change circumstances with your prayers and help create situations that will bring a person into contact with the Lord. In Luke 10:2, Jesus instructed us to "pray ye therefore the Lord of the harvest, that he would send forth laborers into His harvest." You just need to ask God to send born-again, spirit-filled, holy, righteous, justified, Word-believing people across the paths of those you are praying for. You have the authority to interfere with the assignments of those spirits: " the god of this world that hath blinded the minds of them which believe not, least the light of the glorious gospel of Christ, who is the image of God, should shine unto them" (II Corinthians 4:4).

Remember: "We wrestle not against flesh and blood, but against principalities, against powers, against the rulers of the darkness of this world, against spiritual wickedness in high places" (Ephesians 6:12).

The devils and demon spirits can only do what you allow them to do; we are told in Colossians 2:10 that we "are complete in Him [in Christ], which is the head of all principality and power." And Ephesians 1:3 tells us that we "have been blessed with all spiritual blessings in heavenly places in Christ." Remember that God has also given us authority to trample on "serpents and scorpions and over all the power of the enemy" (Luke 10:19).

God Himself is the power, the force, behind this authority. You and I, the believers, when we are fully conscious of this divine authority, can therefore face the enemy without fear or hesitation. For behind the authority possessed by us, the believer is a power far greater than the power of the devil and his crowd. And they are compelled to recognize that authority.

So now you can clean your house and be rid of those demonic spirits that are oppressing you and your family. You have God living on the inside of you, and you have all the power and authority he has delegated to you. You have that God-given authority, and when you act in faith based on God's Word, He will back you up all the way.

And then pray the Ephesians 1:16–21 prayer for those on your prayer list by using their name where it says *you, your,* and *ye.*

> I cease not to give thanks for you, making mention of you in my prayers;
> That the God of our Lord Jesus Christ, the Father of glory, may give unto you the spirit of wisdom and revelation in the knowledge of him:
> The eyes of your understanding being enlightened; that ye may know what is the hope of his calling, and what the riches of the glory of his inheritance in the Saints.
> And what is the exceeding greatness of his power to us-ward who believe, according to the working of his mighty power
> Which he wrought in Christ, when he raised him from the dead and set him at his own right hand in the heavenly places.
> In Jesus' Name.

I encourage you to say this prayer for yourself also so that the revelation of God's Word will begin to come to you.

A second prayer that I encourage you to say, for yourself and others, is from Ephesians 3:14–21. Stay at it, because it won't work if you pray it on a hit-or-miss basis. Do it morning and night, and more frequently if you can.

> For this cause I bow my knees unto the Father of our lord Jesus Christ,
> Of whom the whole family in heaven and earth is named,
> That he would grant you according to the riches of his glory, to be strengthened with might by His Spirit in their inner man;
> That Christ may dwell in your hearts by faith; that you being rooted and grounded in love,

May be able to comprehend with all saints what is the breadth, and length, and depth, and height;

And to know the love of Christ, which passeth knowledge, that you might be filled with all the fullness of God.

Now unto him that is able to do exceeding abundantly above all that we ask or think, *according to the power that worketh in us,*

Unto him be glory in the church by Christ Jesus throughout all ages, would without end. Amen.

That power referred to here is your faith, and you release your faith by speaking out God's Word. The Word of God conceived in the heart, formed by the tongue, and spoken out of the mouth is creative power.

My prayer for you also includes this, from Colossians 1:9–11:

I pray that you might be filled with the knowledge of his will in all wisdom and spiritual understanding;

That you might walk worthy of the Lord unto all pleasing, being fruitful in every good work, and increasing in the knowledge of God. Strengthened with all might according to his glorious power unto all patience and longsuffering with joyfulness. In Jesus' Name.

Two additional verses that you should take notice of are James 5:16 and Isaiah 55:11 (AMP). In Isaiah, God is telling us, "His Word that goes forth out of your mouth: shall not return to Him void [without producing any effect, being useless], but it shall accomplish that which I please and purpose, and it shall prosper in the thing for which He sent it." And James 5:16 tells us, "The earnest (heartfelt, *continued*) prayer of a righteousness man makes tremendous power available [dynamic in its working]."

Be encouraged, because your time spent in prayer is never wasted. Always start or end your prayer with the Name of Jesus. When you speak that Name, you will always get God's attention (John 14:13, 15:16, 16:23).

15

PRAISE GOD AND GIVE THANKS IN ALL THINGS

Giving praise and thanksgiving is the key to releasing God's supernatural power in your life. You must give God the praise before victory comes (Ephesians 5:20; Colossians 3:17; I Thessalonians 5:18).

> (Psalm 34:1): I will bless the Lord at all times: his praise shall continually be in my mouth.
>
> (Psalm 22:3): But thou art holy, O thou that inhabitest the praises of Israel.
>
> (Psalms 67:5-6): Let the people praise thee, O God: let all the people praise thee. Then shall the earth yield her increase; and God, even our own God, shall bless thee.
>
> (Psalm 119:164): Seven times a day do I praise thee because of thy righteousness judgments.

The Word of God is forever settled in heaven, and it is up to you to establish His Word here on the earth (Psalms 119:89).

When you begin to say what God says about you in His Word, you get into agreement with Him. And the more positive that the words you speak about yourself are, the healthier your self-image will be. And the higher that your thoughts are in Jesus, the greater His power is over your soul.

It is the Word of God that is conceived in your heart, formed by your tongue, and spoken out of your mouth that becomes creative power. As you give voice to God's Word, the law of the Spirit of life in Christ Jesus will be energized. It will break you free from the law of sin and death, and it will allow God's life in you to energize or quicken every cell of your body (Romans 8:2, 11).

Ephesians 5:1 directs us to "Be ye therefore followers of God, as dear children." The word *followers*, from the Greek *mimeetees, mimeetou, ho*, means to imitate. We are to imitate God As a child does his or her parents. When you see a boy imitating his father, he walks like him, talks like him, and patterns his every move after him. And it is the same with girls. What is amazing to me is why so many parents can't figure why their children act the way that they do when they are simply imitating them.

In the same respect, read through the four Gospels and mark everything that Jesus said and everything that He did. Notice that He spent much time in prayer, and He always prayed the answer, never the problem. He always based His words on what God had already said about the situation, spoke about what the end results would be, and He used the written Word to defeat the devil at every turn

The following are confessions of faith that I have put together over the years, and I use them to start the day off with a positive frame of mind or to encourage myself in the lord to pick me up when I feel down.

Any time that you are down and need a pick-me-up just start praising God by reading the following verses out loud. As you do, you are calling those things in your life that be not as though they were. You are using God's Word to call into reality those things that you do not have yet. As you meditate on God's Word, you will realize that God has already established those things by promise, but you have to call them into reality by mixing your faith with God's Word.

These are the principles that Paul is giving us insight into in I Corinthians 1:27–28 (AMP):

> [No] for God selected (deliberately chose) what in the world is foolish to put the wise to shame, and what the world calls weak to put the strong to shame.
>
> And God also selected (deliberately chose) what in the world is lowborn and insignificant and branded and treated with contempt, even the things that are nothing, that He might depose and bring to nothing the things that are.

In short, God uses spiritual forces which are not seen to nullify natural things that are seen. This is the Bible principle of calling things that are not as though they were.

Anytime that God quickens a verse or several verses to you, you can simply turn them into a faith-building confession by putting yourself into the verses. As an example, I am going to use the first two verses of Psalms 91. When I started this, I was simply calling those things that were not as though they were.

> He that dwelleth in the secret place of the most High shall abide under the shadow of the Almighty.
> I say of You Lord, He is my refuge and my fortress: my God; in him will I trust (Psalm 91:1-2).

I honestly did not know what those verses were telling me when I started confessing them, but I relied on the Holy Spirit to bring me into all truth and give me a full understanding (revelation knowledge), and I now live under the shadow of the Almighty. The Holy Spirit also showed how to take those words and make them personal just for me.

The 91ˢᵗ Psalm in its entirety is printed out at the end of this chapter and I recommend that you come to know every word of it by heart so that at any time even the thought of any danger or harm comes near to you, it will flow from your lips without you even thinking about it. That is what causes the power of God to be at your disposal at a moment's notice!

As you read the following confessions, stop and think about what God is saying to you. Spend a few minutes praying in the Holy Spirit and allow Him to bring you into all truth, give you revelation knowledge as to what the Father is telling you, and show you how to change your life to allow you to become the person that He wants you to be.

Using this principle has changed me to such an extent that God is now able to use me to write these books, which now enable many thousands of men and women to come into a closer walk with Him.

The following verses are the ones that I have used for my spiritual growth, but other lists can be made up for the healing of your body based on Isaiah 53:4–5, I Peter 2:24, and Matthew 8:17 or for material needs based on Philippians 4:19, Galatians 3:13, Deuteronomy 28, Isaiah 53:5–6, John 10:10, and John 5:24, and so on.

There are many other subjects and verses to go with them, but it is up to you to dig them out and put them together for your benefit. Remember that the Holy Spirit is in you to bring you into all truth. You simply have to allow Him to do it for you.

Look for books titled "God's Promises for You" or "God's Creative Power" at your local Christian book store as they would be a great help getting you started. Don't just read the words, but digest them and what they are saying and apply them to your life. Jesus said in Matthew 7:24-27,

Therefore whosoever heareth these sayings of mine, and doeth them, I will liken him unto a wise man, which built his house upon a rock; And the rain descended, and the floods came, and the winds blew, and beat upon that house; and it fell not: for it was founded upon a rock. And every one that heareth these sayings of mine, and doeth them not, shall be likened unto a foolish man, which built his house upon the sand: And the rain descended, and the floods came, and it fell: and great was the fall of it.

Jesus is telling us here that the man who built his house on the sand is the man who has heard the Word but didn't do anything about it. But the man who built his hose on the rock is the man who heard the Word and did something about it. He spent quality time in the Word until it became the *rema* Word to him.

Don't be just a hearer of the Word but also a doer. If you're not a doer of the Word, you don't have any foundation under you. If you intend to wait until you need faith to get it, you will soon find out that you are too late! That is why I am encouraging you to study the Word for yourself and find out what it says before you need it. The benefit to you is that you will soon find out that you will be blessed in every area of your life.

Note: In Romans 10:9 and Psalms 118:24 the word *Lord* refers to His Majesty, Honor, Authority and Sovereignty].

A PRAYER TO START YOUR DAY

Good morning, Lord Jesus, for this day I again declare that you are my Lord, and I submit this day and all that it contains to you. "For this is the day that the Lord has made, I will rejoice and be glad in it. For the joy of the Lord is my strength, and I am strong in the Lord and the power of His might I can do all things through Christ [The anointed one] who strengthens me." For God is at work in me, creating in me the power and the desire, both to will and to work for His good pleasure (Romans 10:9; Psalms 27:14, 118:24; Nehemiah 8:10; Ephesians 6:10; Philippians 2:13, 4:13).

I have been made in the God class! You, Lord, have placed your life in me and I am dominated by spiritual glow, for I now walk in the light of life, and the life which I now live in the flesh I live by the faith of the Son of God who loved me and gave himself for me. (Genesis 1:26; Galatians 2:20; John 8:12).

"In Him was life, and that life was the light of man." That life is my pathway to manifest goodness, that life is in me, and that life is developing my spirit. I am anointed of God, and I have the mind of Christ; I have the same anointing on my mind that Jesus has on His mind. I am strengthened with might by God's Spirit in my inner man, and I have the wisdom of God, and revelation knowledge flows into me continually, For Jesus is my wisdom. "Jesus has been made unto me wisdom, righteousness, sanctification, and redemption, and I have been made the righteousness of God in Christ Jesus." I have been reconciled to right standing with Almighty God and I have the authority and the right to stand in the Father's presence without a sense of guilt, fear, or inferiority and to talk to Him just like I would talk to my own earthly father (John 1:4; I John 1:5; Colossians 1:11; Ephesians 1:17; I Corinthians 2:16; Philippians 2:5; I Corinthians 1:30; II Corinthians 5:21; Romans 3:2).

And now, "Greater is He that is in me than he that is in me than he that is in the world and I am complete in Him who is the head of all principality and power. Jesus has given me power [authority] over serpents and scorpions and over all the powers of the enemy, and nothing shall by any means hurt me" (I John 4:4; Colossians 2:10; Luke 10:19).

The Greater One lives on the inside of me, and I am a world overcomer! That same power that raised Jesus from the dead now lives in me and is at my disposal twenty-four hours a day, and that anointing, that burden-removing, yoke-destroying power of God that was on Jesus, now lives in me! (I John 2:27, 4:4, 5:4; Romans 8:11).

The devil is a thief and a liar; I will not let him defeat me. I will not let the devil rob me of the blessings of God. Instead, I will walk in faith, the favor of God, and the comfort of the Holy Ghost.

It is not I who live but Christ, the power and the wisdom of God and that anointing [that burden removing and yoke destroying power of God] that I have received of Him that lives in me for I am a new creature in Christ Jesus, that old sin nature has passed away, behold, all things are become new. (Galatians 2:20; I Corinthians 1:24; Colossians 2:3; Isaiah 10:27; I John 2:27; II Corinthians 5:17).

I am an ambassador for Christ representing the Kingdom of God with the fullness of the godhead living in me. I am strong in the Lord and the power of His might, and these signs do follow me (II Corinthians 5:20; Colossians 2:9; Ephesians 6:10).

In Jesus' Name, I cast out devils. I speak with new tongues. I take up serpents, and if I drink any deadly thing, it shall not hurt me.

And when I lay hands on the sick, they shall recover. (Mark 16:16–18).

For it is not I that do these things but You, Lord, for "according to Your divine power, You have given unto me all things that pertain unto life and godliness that I might partake in Your divine nature." I give you all the glory, honor, and praise for it Father, because I choose to believe that "the things that Jesus did I shall do also. And greater works shall I do, because Jesus now sits at the right hand of the Father.

GOD IS A GOOD GOD.

Father, whatever I ask of You in Jesus' Name will be given to me, for all things are possible to me because I believe that I receive them and I am fully persuaded that what You have promised me, you are able to perform. In Jesus' Name (2 Peter 1:3–4; John 14:13–14; Ephesians 1:20; John 16:23; Mark 9:23, 11:23; Romans 4:21).

By faith I walk in God's authority—by His command and In the Name of Jesus. God needs me to love; He needs me in faith, for faith is the divine connection to the creative force of Almighty God, and it works in me by love.

My faith is not just words, but it is what I believe and what I will act upon. It is what is in abundance in my heart that will carry the day for me in a time of trouble.

Without me keeping the love commandment, fear will become the dominate force in my life. Fear causes offence and timidity, and it will cause the blessings of God to be choked off from my life to where they will become unfruitful.

I choose to change my lifestyle to fit the commandment to love, and I have no excuse to violate the commandment to love God and my neighbor as myself. I have the faith, and I am willing to step up and step out and do what God is asking of me.

I release my faith for God's protection and, I say of you, Lord, You are my refuge, You are my fortress, You are my God, and I trust in You. No weapon that is formed against me shall prosper, and nothing shall by any means hurt me; no accident shall overtake me, and no plague shall come near my dwelling.

I praise You, Almighty God, for who You are and all the things you have done for me (Psalms 91:2; Isaiah 54:17; Luke 10:19; Psalms 91:10).

Jesus is Lord over my life: physically, financially, socially, spiritually, and mentally.

Father, I love you with all of my heart, all of my soul, all of my mind, and all of my strength, and I love my neighbor as myself. I thank you, Lord, for loving me just as much as You love Jesus, and I receive Your love for me today (John 17:23).

"For the Lord is good, and His mercy endureth forever." God's goodness and His mercy are with me all of the days of my life (Nahum 1:7; Psalms 100:5, 106:1, 107:1, 136:1–26).

God is pouring upon me the Spirit of grace and I am anointed to do exceedingly, abundantly above all that I could imagine, because I have availed myself to be a good steward of the gift (Zachariah 12:10; Proverbs 3:5).

Lord, I am grateful to have You live and bring Your fullness into my life. For God is good to [your name], and His tender mercies are over me. The Lord is blessing me and keeping me. The Lord makes His face shine upon me and is gracious unto me. The Lord has lifted up his countenance upon me and has given me peace (Colossians 2:9; Numbers 6:24–26; Psalms 145:9).

GOD'S FAVOR IS UPON ME

Thou shalt arise and have mercy upon [your name], for the time to favor him, yea, the set time, is come. The set time to favor me has come. I walk in the favor of God and the comfort of the Holy Ghost. Now, that's the grace of God, for my God is no respecter of persons. God's divine influence is upon my heart, and the reflection of that influence is in my life (Psalms 90:17, 102:13; Proverbs 16:15, 22:1; II Corinthians 5:20).

I am blessed (I am empowered to prosper) and highly favored. I am blessed because I trust in the Lord, and I have confidence in Him. The Lord calls me blessed, and so I am. I am planted firmly in rich soil as I trust in God. I let my confidence in God's Word grow deeper and higher as I ground myself in God's truth [Word] and establish myself in God's love. I am prosperous, I am successful, and I am healthy (Proverbs 3:3–4; II Corinthians 12:9; Jeremiah 17:7).

The favor of God surrounds me like a shield, and everything I touch prospers and succeeds. That success is my fulfilling the plan that God has placed in my life. For the same favor that was upon Joseph is upon me (Joshua 1:5; Proverbs 3:3, 4; Genesis 41:40).

I claim God's favor by faith, and I anticipate the favor of God going before me and surrounding me. I expect to be supported, endorsed, and assisted; to have things made easier for me; to be provided with advantages; and to be shown special privileges. I expect God to open doors for me that no man or the devil can shut (Revelation 3:8).

The divine favor of God is on my life, and I am free from fear. I will not fear because God has given me the spirit of power and of love, and a sound mind and perfect love cast out all fear (II Timothy 1:7; I John 4:8).

It is good for me to draw near to God for I have put my trust in the Lord and have made Him my refuge and my fortress that I may tell of all His good works (Psalms 73:28, 91:2).

God is love. He lives in me, and I choose to love others. Therefore, I am not boastful or vainglorious. I do not display myself haughtily. I am not conceited, arrogant, or inflated with pride. I am not rude. I am not unmannerly. I do not act unbecomingly. I act in love (I Corinthians 13:4–5; I John 4:8, 16).

I declare jubilee over my life today, because I have a repentant heart, and I am growing up to be the man that God wants me to be. I am walking in God's perfect will for my life (Mark 11:23).

I am blessed with all spiritual blessings in heavenly places in Christ and with all things that pertain unto life and godliness. I live in divine health and am free from debt so that I in turn can be A blessing to everyone else (Mark 11:23; Jeremiah 29:11; I Peter 3:12).

I am becoming more God-inside-me-minded, and I am developing an awareness of the reality of the Holy Spirit within me. It is not in my ability to please God but in God's ability in me, and it is my responsibility to quit trying and surrender everything to Him (Philippians 2:13; Mark 11:23).

LIGHT SPEAKS OF THE POWER AND THE LIFE OF GOD'S NATURE

"In Him was life,* and that life was the light of man." That light is my pathway to manifest goodness. That light is the manifest presence of God living on the inside of me, and that life is developing my spirit (John 8:12, 14:23, 17:23; Psalms 112:4).

I have an unction (anointing, wisdom) to know all things (I John 2:20). I am being strengthened with might by God's Spirit in my inner man, and I have the wisdom of God, and revelation knowledge flows into me continually (Proverbs 20:27; John 1:4; I John 1:5; Malachi 4:1–2; John 5:26, 8:12, 14:23, 17:23; Psalms 112:4; I John 2:20; James 1:5; Matthew 16:18; I Corinthians 1:30; Ephesians 1:17, 2:16).

Jesus is my wisdom. Jesus has been made unto me wisdom, righteousness, sanctification, and redemption (I Corinthians 1:30; Romans 8:32). I have been made the righteousness of God in Christ Jesus, and I have the right to stand in the Father's presence without a sense of fear, guilt, or inferiority and talk to Him like I would talk to my earthly father (II Corinthians 5:21).

I live by the revelation of who I am in the presence of God. I am in the Word of God, and God is revealing Himself to me. Because He is in me, God knows everything that I am going through. Because He loves me, He has given me the ability to know all that He knows. And now greater is He that is in me than he that is in the world (I John 4:4; I Corinthians 6:19–20).

(*The word *life* here in the Greek is *zoe*, which means eternal life, or God's life. It is God's nature. It is life as God has it—that which the Father has in Himself—and that which the Incarnate Son has in Himself. It is called eternal life, everlasting life, and sometimes just life.

It is that life that one receives when they make Jesus their lord and Savior. It is what the Word is referring to when it says that you are *in Him* or *in Christ*.) (II Corinthians 5:17-21.)

GOD'S LOVE FOR ME

Greater is the love that is in me than the fear that is in the world (II Corinthians 6:16–18).

God is light, and God is life and God is love and He loves me as much as He loves Jesus, for I am the focus of God's love (John 4:24, 17:23; I John 1:5, 4:8; Amos 5:4).

It is not I who live, but Christ (the Anointed One and His Anointing) that lives in me, and the life that I now live in the flesh I live by the faith of the Son of God who loved me and gave himself for me (Colossians 2:20).

The Greater One lives in me, and He has given me all the wisdom, strength, power, and provision that I need to crush the devil like a bug, because "He is able to do exceeding abundantly above all that I ask or think, according to the power, my faith that worketh in me." All of heaven is breaking loose in my life, and I expect Him to do wise, wonderful, amazing, and miraculous things through me, because I have chosen to become God-inside-me-minded enough to let that power flow (I John 4:4; Ephesians 3:16–20).

I serve God with gladness and a joyful heart! The joy of the Lord is my strength, and I am strong in the Lord and the power of His might (Deuteronomy 28:47; Nehemiah 8:10; Ephesians 6:10).

Because the Spirit of him that raised up Jesus from the dead lives in me, He that raised up Christ from the dead is also quickening (making alive) my mortal body by His Spirit that lives in me. (Romans 8:11) For in him dwelleth all the fullness of the Godhead bodily and I am complete in Him, which is the head of all principality and power (Colossians 2:9–10).

"I in them, and thou in me, that they may be made perfect in one; and that the world may know that thou hast sent me, and hath loved them, as thou hast loved me" (John 17:23). That's how much Jesus loves me.

As I become more God-inside-me-minded, my capacity for fullness grows. The fullness of His gifts and calling are overflowing my life, and they are manifesting themselves to the world in love. God loves me just as much as He loves Jesus, and I shall not fear, for I am a fearless, faith-filled sower of love, and I am a reaper of love's full abundance. This is my year of the fullness of God, and I will walk in it for the rest of my life (Ephesians 1:23).

GOD'S GLORY IN ME

To God be all the glory, praise, and honor! I am so glad that the glory is here!

"That anointing (That burden-removing, yoke-destroying power of God) that I have received of Him abides (lives) in me" so that I can dispense that gift to others (John 15:7; Isaiah 10:27; I John 2:27).

I am one with God, I am clothed in His glory, and I have the mind of Christ (The Anointed One). I have that same anointing on my mind that Jesus has on His mind (John 17:22; I Corinthians 2:16; Philippians 2:5). For "In Him (In Christ) dwelleth all the fullness of the Godhead bodily. And I am complete in Him, which is the head of all principality and power" (Colossians 2:9–10).

In Christ, I, too, am filled with the Godhead: Father, Son, and Holy Spirit, and I am reaching full spiritual stature (Luke 10:19).

Jesus has given me power to tread on serpents and scorpions and over all the power of the enemy, and nothing shall by any means hurt me. As a believer, one who adheres to, trusts in, and relies on the Gospel and Him whom it sets forth, In Jesus' Name I cast out devils. I speak with new tongues. I take up serpents, and if I drink any deadly thing, it shall not hurt me. And when I lay hands on the sick, they shall recover. (Philippians 2:9–10; Mark 16:17–18)

I am a citizen of heaven and an ambassador for Christ, and I expect these things to happen because I am a son of God. I know who I am in Christ, and I have the spirit of excellence in my life. The works that He did shall I do also, and greater works than these shall I do, because He went to His father. And I am well able to fulfill my destiny, because I also sit together in heavenly places in Christ Jesus (Ephesians 2:6; II Corinthians 5:20; Galatians 4:7; John 1:12).

"My God is able to do exceeding abundantly above all that I ask or think, according to the power, the anointing, that works in me"
(Mark 11:24; II Timothy 1:7; John 14:12; II Corinthians 5:20; Ephesians 1:20, 2:6; Romans 8:14, 18; I John 2:27).

Because I live in the faith zone, I exercise my faith to please God. (Revelation 4:11).

My faith is based on my relationship with God and I choose to keep myself in the love of God. (Jude 21; Ephesians 5:2).

I have been made the righteousness of God in Christ Jesus.
I am in "right standing with God". (II Corinthians 5:21). Jesus has given me the right to speak His Word in His Name and by His blood and stand in equality with Him (Matthew 28:18–20; Philippians 2:6).

I have an authority and a right to stand in the Father's presence without the sense of sin, guilt, fear, inferiority, or condemnation and to talk to Him just like I would talk to my own earthly father (Hebrews 4:16).

Their righteousness is of me, saith the Lord!

Father, I thank You for Your promises. I praise You that You are the Lord, my Redeemer. Your kindness and the covenant of Your peace shall never depart from me.

All my borders are laid with pleasant stones. All my children are taught of You and great is the peace of my children.

I am established in Your righteousness. Even though fear, oppression, and terror shall gather together, they are not from You. I'll not receive them! They shall fall for my sake!

Fall, fear! Fall, oppression! Fall, terror! You're not from God, and you'll not come near me! Jesus has defeated the devil and all of his works.

No weapon formed against me shall prosper!

*Every tongue that rises against me shall be condemned. This is my inheritance and my blood-bought right in Jesus. He is my righteousness.

The Word (Jesus) says so! (Isaiah 54:8–17; I Peter 3:12).

*"… and every tongue that shall rise against you in judgment you shall show to be in the wrong. This [peace, righteousness, security, triumph over opposition] is the heritage of the servants of the Lord [those in whom the Ideal Servant of the Lord is reproduced]; this is the righteousness or the

vindication which they obtain from Me [this is that which I impart to them as their justification], says the Lord" (Isaiah 54:17 AMP).

THE PROSPERITY PROFILE OF THE RIGHTEOUS

"I praise you, Lord! Blessed, happy, and fortunate [to be envied] am I, the man who fears (reveres and worships) You, Lord, and who delights greatly in Your commandments.

My seed shall be mighty upon the earth: the generation of the upright shall be blessed. Wealth and riches are coming into my house, and my righteousness endures forever.

Unto the upright there arises light in the darkness; I am gracious and full of compassion and righteous. A good man showeth favor and lendeth; I guide my affairs with discretion. I shall not be moved forever; the righteous shall be in everlasting remembrance.

I am not afraid of evil tidings; my heart is fixed, trusting in You, Lord. My heart is established and steady (fixed). I am not afraid, while I wait to see my desire upon my enemies.

I have dispersed, and I have given to the poor; my righteousness endures forever, and my horn is being exalted with honor. The wicked shall see it and be grieved; he shall gnash with his teeth and melt away; the desire of the wicked shall perish" (Psalms 112 AMP).

Because I am in Christ and Christ is in me, I walk in liberty, and I can do all things through Christ who strengthens me (Galatians 2:20; II Corinthians 3:17; Galatians 2:4; Philippians 4:13). I am more than a conquer through Him who loved us (Romans 8:37). And I always triumph over opposition (II Corinthians 2:14). For the earth is the Lord's and the fullness therein (Psalms 24:1).

Because I place my higher thoughts in Jesus, the greater is God's power over my soul. (My mind and thoughts, my will and my emotions) (Habakkuk 3:19).

I am a born-again, spirit-filled, holy, righteous, justified, anointed, son of God (Romans 10:9; I Corinthians 3:16; Romans 11:16; II Corinthians 5:21; Romans 8:33; I John 2:27; Romans 8:14).

I am born of God and overcometh the world, because I believe and confess that Jesus is the Son of God (I John 5:4–5; Revelation 12:11; Romans 8:15).

I overcome the world, the flesh, and the devil by the blood of the Lamb and the word of my testimony (I John 4:4; Revelation 12:11).

I am a covenant son, an heir of God, and a joint heir with Christ. I am a joint heir with Jesus, who was appointed heir of all things, and I am an heir to the anointing that's on the anointed One, and as a joint heir I am an equal heir. (Hebrews 1:2; Titus 3:7; I John 3:2; Romans 8:17).

I have the same rights that Christ (the Anointed One) has in His inheritance.

I have inherited His anointing and the right to walk in the benefits that come from being anointed.

I have the same privileges and the same rights;

That's why I am a member of the body of Christ, or the body of the Anointed One and His anointing (I Corinthians 12:27).

I expect God's glory on me! He's my Father! He has taken my cares (John 17:22). I have taken His Name, His Spirit, His Word, His blood, and His Anointing, and all of heaven is mine. I've been set free from the kingdom of darkness, and I live in the Kingdom of God's dear Son, Jesus.

He's my Lord and my Savior, and I have inherited His:

Wisdom Anointing: God's ability to use knowledge.

Understanding Anointing: The ability to know how God sees things and have insight into His ways.

Spirit of counsel: Having someone who knows everything to counsel me in every matter so that I deal wisely in every affair of life.

Spirit of Might: The ability to walk in God's weapons, which are not carnal but mighty for the pulling down of strongholds.

Spirit of Knowledge: The mind of Christ—the same anointing on my mind that Jesus walked in when He was on the earth.

Spirit of the fear of the Lord: The anointing of honor and understanding of blood covenant relationship with God. (Isaiah 11:2)

These anointings are making me of quick understanding in the fear of You, Lord. That's the anointing to understand quickly, at the moment I need to know, how the Kingdom of God operates and how to defeat the devil and his crowd right on the spot.

I walk in truth, in the light of God's Word, according to His ways and His wisdom. I know the truth, and the truth is making me free (John 8:31–32).

I prosper as my soul prospers in understanding of the Word of God (3 John 2).

I live a godly lifestyle, in obedience to what God says is right, and because I am willing and obedient, I eat the good of the land (Isaiah 1:19).

Because I fear the Lord, He teaches me how to choose the best, and I live within His circle of blessing (Psalms 25:12–13).

I separate myself from darkness, and God is a Father to me (II Corinthians 6:17–18).

His truth (word) is my shield and my buckler (armor) (Psalms 91:4).

I walk in faithfulness, and I am blessed, because I constantly do what is right (Psalms 106:3).

I receive what I ask for from God, because I watchfully obey His instructions and habitually practice what is pleasing to Him (I John 3:22).

I abound with blessings, because I am faithful (Proverbs 28:20).

I walk in diligence and obey God's commands, and His blessings overtake me (Deuteronomy 28:1–2).

I am blessed and highly favored of God, and I am living in all the fullness of God (Ephesians 3:19).

God rewards me, because I diligently seek Him (Hebrews 11:6).

I honor the Lord by bringing Him all of my tithe and my storage places are filled with plenty. God has opened the windows of heaven and is blessing me so there is not room enough for me to receive it all, and He has rebuked the devourer for my sake (Malachi 3:10–11).

I sow bountifully, therefore I reap bountifully. I am a cheerful giver, and it is given back to me in good measure, pressed down, shaken together, and running over (2 Corinthians 9:6–8; Luke 6:38).

I receive my daily bread according to I Corinthians 9:10. I receive my seed sown multiplied so that I can be sufficient and give more.

I am anointed to get wealth (Deuteronomy 8:18).

I believe, therefore I say what God says. I am of faith, so I am blessed like faithful Abraham (II Corinthians 4:13; Galatians 3:9; Jude 3).

The word of faith is in my heart and in my mouth, because I earnestly contend for the faith that was once delivered unto the saints. I tell the mountains in my life to be removed and cast into the sea. I believe that those things I say shall come to pass, so I have whatsoever I say (Romans 10:8; Mark 11:24).

"And it is coming to pass, because I hearken diligently unto the voice of the Lord my God, to observe and do all His commandments that He has commanded me this day, that the Lord my God has set me on high above all the nations of the earth:

And all these blessings come on me and are overtaking me, because I hearken unto the voice of the Lord my God.

Blessed am I in the city, and blessed am I in the field.

Blessed is the fruit of my body, the fruit of my ground, the fruit of my cattle, the increase of my kine, and the flocks of my sheep.

Blessed am I in my basket and my store.

Blessed am I when I come in, and blessed am I when I go out (Deuteronomy 28:1–6).

Father, according to Ephesians 1:16–23, You have given me the spirit of wisdom and revelation of Jesus Christ. I thank You that the eyes of my understanding are being enlightened to know the hope of Your calling and the riches of the glory of Your inheritance in the saints. You are revealing to me the exceeding greatness of Your power, according to the working of Your mighty power, which raised Christ from the dead and set Him at your right hand. I receive all these benefit in Jesus' name.

I speak these things out from a godly or spiritual standpoint, and I expect to see these things happen, because my words carry power. I am operating in faith and the knowledge and understanding of my inheritance in Christ Jesus, and this earthly system has to obey me as I put a demand on the covenant that I have with Almighty God.

I believe that I receive these things based on God's word: "What things soever you desire when you pray, believe that you receive them, and you shall have them. In Jesus' Name" (Mark 11:24).

Thank you, Lord, for teaching me to profit, for leading me in the way that I should go, and always causing me to triumph in Christ Jesus, because I hearken to the commandments of my Lord (II Corinthians 2:14; Isaiah 48:17).

GOD IS DOING A NEW THING IN MY LIFE

"Remember ye not the former things, neither consider the things of old. Behold, I am doing a new thing" (Isaiah 43:18–19).

Lord, I stir myself up to be ready to be used—an end-time servant—to open my mouth and declare the wonderful works of God. Help me ready myself for Your service so that Your perfect will be done in me and in my life.

My life will no longer be ordinary. Something new, out of the ordinary is happening. I am seeing wonderful and strange and incredible and unthinkable things today!

God is taking me to another level, and is causing me to believe things about God that I have never been able to believe before.

He is taking me beyond what I have been capable of thinking or imagining in the past. He is opening the door to a whole new realm of possibilities for my life. For all things are possible to me because I believe that those things that I say shall come to pass (I Timothy 1:6; Mark 9:23, 11:23).

God has removed my past limitations from my mind. What I could not think yesterday, I can now think today. God wants me to think about Him doing the things that I could not imagine Him doing yesterday. The more I see God do what men don't think He can do, the bigger my thoughts will become. I'm a much bigger thinker today than I was yesterday, and my thoughts will be much bigger tomorrow, because I have an anointing to know all things.

Enlarge the place of thy tent and let them stretch forth the curtains of thine habitations; spare not, lengthen thy cords, and strengthen thy stakes (Isaiah 54:2).

GOD IS CHANGING MY WAYS OF THINKING

"For my thoughts are not your thoughts, neither are your ways my ways, saith the Lord. For as the heavens are higher than the earth, so are my ways higher than your ways, and my thoughts than your thoughts" (Isaiah 55:8–9).

"O Lord, how great are thy works; and thy thoughts are very deep" (Psalms 92:5).

"The thoughts of the diligent tend only to plenteous" (Proverbs 21:5).

God is telling me: You've seen what I've done in your life in the past, now go with me to the next level. Enlarge your thinking, stretch your thinking, and spare not in your thinking. Don't limit me; think the unthinkable. In conclusion, God is bringing me up to His level of thinking, and my thoughts are going to become higher and deeper. Lack will no longer be in my thinking; I'll think plenty, abundance, and more than enough.

God is removing from my mind my past limitations. What I couldn't think yesterday, I'll be able to think today! My life is going in the direction of my most dominant thoughts. I am thinking the unthinkable.

No other generation has been able to think the thoughts that I will think.

Arise, shine, for thy light is come, and the glory [material wealth and blessings] of the Lord has risen upon [your name]. For behold, the darkness shall cover the earth, and gross darkness the people: but the Lord shall arise upon [your name], and his glory shall be seen upon [your name]. And the gentiles shall come to [your name]'s light, and kings to the brightness of [your name]'s rising (Isaiah 60:1–3).

For thou, Lord, will bless the righteous; with favor wilt thou compass [your name] as with a shield (Psalms 5:12). God's glory is being seen upon me. God's favor is bringing about increase.

"Then thou shalt see, and flow together, and thine heart shall fear, and be enlarged; because the abundance of the sea [the mass people of the earth] shall be converted unto [your name], the forces of the Gentiles shall come unto [your name]. Therefore thy gates shall be open continually; they shall not be shut day nor night; that men may bring unto [your name] the forces of the Gentiles" (Isaiah 60:5–11).

This is our "exceeding abundantly above all that we ask or think" time. God has given us the heritage of the heathen (Psalms 111:6).

"But you shall be named the Priests of the Lord: men shall call you the Ministers of our God: You shall eat the riches, and in their glory shall you boast yourselves.

For your shame you shall have double; and for confusion they shall rejoice in their portion: therefore in their land they shall possess the double: everlasting joy shall be unto them.

For I the Lord love judgment, I hate robbery for burnt offering; and I will direct their work in truth, and I will make an everlasting covenant with them.

And their seed shall be known among the Gentiles, and their offspring among the people: all that see them shall acknowledge them, that they are the seed which the Lord hath blessed" (Isaiah 61:6–9).

I WALK IN A DOUBLE PORTION OF INHERITANCE, FAVOR, HONOR, AND GOD'S ANOINTING

"Behold, I will make [your name] a new sharp threshing instrument having teeth: thou shalt thresh the mountains, and beat them small, and shalt make the hills as chaff.

[Your name] shalt fan them, and the wind shall carry them away, and the whirlwind shall scatter them: and [your name] shalt rejoice in the Lord, and shalt glory in the Holy One of Israel" (Isaiah 41:15–16).

"The Lord is protecting [your name] from all dangers: And He is guarding [your name]'s life" (Psalms 121:7).

"God is bringing to light what is hidden in darkness, and exposing the motives of men's hearts" (I Corinthians 4:5).

"The Lord is my refuge and my fortress: my God; in Him do I trust" (Psalms 91:2).

God is my source, so I expect the blessing to be manifested in my life, I expect God to do the extraordinary. (Galatians 3:14).

PSALMS 103:3–8 (my translation)

Lord, in obedience to Your Word, I recall and receive anew today all the benefits that Jesus has provided for me.

1. You have forgiven all my sins.
2. You are my healer, and I receive my healing and health today.
3. My life is redeemed from destruction.
4. I am crowned with Your loving-kindness and tender mercies.
5. You satisfy my mouth with good things so that my youth is renewed like the eagles.
6. You execute righteousness and judgment for me against oppression. "I'm free."
7. You make known Your ways to me. I am Your child, and I follow You.
8. I receive Your grace and mercy and obtain it in times of need.

I'm so glad that Jesus did all of that for me.

PSALMS 91 (my translation)

I am he that dwelleth in the secrete place of the most High and I abide under the shadow of the Almighty

I say of You, Lord, You are my refuge and my fortress; You are my God; it is in You that I place my trust.

For You have delivered me from the snare of the fowler and from the noisome pestilence.

You are covering me with Your feathers, and under Your wings do I trust: Your truth (word) is my shield and my buckler.

I am not afraid for the terror by night; nor for the arrow that flieth by day.

Nor for the pestilence that walketh in darkness; nor for the destruction and sudden death that surprise and lay waste at noonday.

A thousand shall fall at my side and ten thousand at my right hand, but it shall not come near me.

Only with my eyes shall I behold and see the reward of the wicked.

Because I have made You, Lord, which is my refuge, even the most High, my habitation.

There shall be no accident befall me, neither shall any plague come near my dwelling.

For You, Lord, have given Your angles charge over me to keep me in all my ways.

They are bearing me up in their hands, lest I dash my foot against a stone.

I shall tread upon the lion and adder: the young lion and the dragon shall I trample under my feet.

Because I have set my love upon You, Almighty God, You have delivered me: You have set me on high, because I know Your name.

When I call upon You, You always answer me; You are with me in trouble; You are delivering me and honoring me.

With long life are You satisfying me, and showing me my salvation.

Note: Salvation from the Greek and Hebrew implies the ideas of material and temporal deliverance from danger and apprehension, safety, preservation, pardon, restoration, healing, wholeness, and soundness [health].

Confess: Because I have set my love upon You Lord, the God who is more than enough, You have shown me Your salvation. You has made known to me the Gospel of Jesus Christ, which is the power of God unto my salvation, deliverance, safety, preservation, healing and my health. (Romans 1:16)

Now faith is being sure of what we hope for and certain of what we do not see (Hebrews 11:1 NIV). This is telling us that even when we do not know and see all the things that have been promised to us – when we have prayed something specific that has not come through to us and it looks in the natural that things are going in the opposite direction we can put our hope and trust in the Lord and expect that He is going to prove Himself faithful on our behalf.

Our responsibility as Christians is to take the responsibility and put our faith in Him, which means that we are to embrace this world's uncertainty in a spirit of expectancy!

God has placed His life in each one of us and He has given us the ability to see the light at the end of the tunnel and to walk through all of our tests and trials that life throws at us without getting a scratch on us.

He created us to walk in faith and shine as His Kingdom ambassadors.

He expects us to call upon Him to do great and awesome feats for us, in us and through us as we carry out the assignment that He has for us in this life.

In Romans 5:17 Paul gives us insight as to what God expects of us.

> For if because of one man's trespass (lapse, offense) death reigned through that one, much more surely will those who receive [God's] overflowing grace (unmerited favor) and the free gift of righteousness [putting them into right standing with Himself] reign as kings in life through the one Man Jesus Christ (the Messiah, the Anointed One). (AMP)

Notice that it does not say that life reigns in us or over us. It says that we shall reign as kings in life! That word *reign* in the Greek, *basileuo,* means: to be king, to exercise kingly power, to govern a province, to exercise the highest influence, to control.

Take a few minutes to study Romans 5:12-21 and see why every believer has the glorious privilege to reign in life as a joint heir with Jesus Himself.

Now is the time for each one of us to step up and step out and be all that God has called us to be.